The Life Of A

Psychic Detective

An Unlimited Mind Publication

Book Cover Design by Amanda Wilson, amandawilsonart.com
Cover Photograph by Anna Ryabtsov, annarybtsov@mail.com
Logo by Julie Bond Genovese, https://nothingshortofjoy.com/
Head Shot by Greg Martz, https://www.inhousenj.com/greg-martz

Revised Edition 2022

Unlimited Mind Publishing
Lightwing Center
PO Box 1132
Denville, NJ 07834
nancyorlenweber.com
nancy@nancyorlenweber.com

Revised Edition Copyright© 2022 by Nancy Orlen Weber
ISBN 978-1-959334-02-6 BOOK
ISBN 978-1-959334-03-3 EBOOK

All rights assigned to Lightwing Center of LifeSpirit Collaborative Congregations. The Assignee reserves all rights. No part of this publication may be reproduced, distributed, or transmitted in any form or by any means, including photocopying, recording, or other electronic or mechanical methods, without the prior written permission of the publisher, except in the case of brief quotations embodied in critical reviews and certain other noncommercial uses permitted by copyright law. For permission requests contact the publisher, "Attention: Permissions Coordinator," by email to lightwingcenter@gmail.com or by mail at the address above.

Ordering Information: Individual paperback and ebooks may be obtained at NancyOrlenWeber.com or online book stores
Personalized Author Signed Books from nancyorlenweber.com on request
Individual books are $12.95, plus applicable taxes and shipping.

A portion of the proceeds from the sale of each book is donated to *The Young Living Foundation's* efforts, in partnership with *Hope For Justice,* dedicated to ending human trafficking.

Ebooks are $8.95

Quantity sales: Special discounts are available on quantity purchases by groups, associations, and others.

For details, contact the publisher at the address above.

Orders by U.S. trade bookstores and wholesalers.
Inquire By Email To: nancy@nancyorlenweber.com
Please note the Subject: PD Books group & bulk sales.

Printed in the United States of America   Printed 2022

Some names were changed to protect their privacy or for the safety of others involved.

"Never doubt that a small group of thoughtful, committed people can change the world; indeed, it's the only thing that ever has."
—Margaret Mead.

THIS BOOK IS DEDICATED
TO ALL THOSE WHO MAKE A DIFFERENCE

To all the authors of the original Nancy Drew books, a big thank you for giving me the courage to be different, to lead rather than follow. On the surface, those books were not intended to do much, yet I believe that the souls of all those who participated knew better. Reading in the 1940s and '50s of a heroine other than Wonder Woman (who I also loved), Nancy Drew was more of a real-life possibility.

To Bill Hughes, who was a detective in Mount Olive when we worked together, went on to work with the state and is now retired. You not only believed in me and allowed me to work with you, but you also agreed to take time to go on the shows and speak openly about working with a psychic. I have come to know your family and will rejoice, always, in our friendship.

To retired Captain of Homicide, Jimmy Moore, your trust of Bill Hughes as a partner on the task force while searching for a serial killer led to our meeting. It was amazing to be in the company of two men who do their work with so much heart and belief in always doing their best. Thank you both for the times we spent together on the job and while filming.

To PI and retired detective, Gary Micco and retired Captain George Deuchar (now Director of Training for PowerPhone, Inc.,) who both took a big leap of faith when they agreed that Det. Micco would meet with me; thank you. This would be the start of many opportunities to work with and learn with them.

To the many law enforcement agents I've worked with locally, throughout the US, and in other countries, federal, local, and international agencies, thank you. While I've learned that I'm a part of the team and sometimes can offer a piece of the puzzle, you chose to seek me out. That validation, for an introverted and shy person, has made it possible for me to do this work.

Thank you also to all the journalists, interviewers, documentary film makers, and any who thought to examine, write, and talk about this work, whether believing or disbelieving. Your probing has helped me gain more insight and more understanding of the importance of keeping the ego in check. Above all, it has demonstrated again and again that the "aha's" never stop. By asking questions about the mechanics, you have helped me create a deeper understanding of the process. Your interest and curiosity have helped me in many ways to refine my own appreciation of the gift. This inward journey requires constant vigilance over my thoughts and the continual release of emotional pain garnered from reaching into both my own traumas and everyone else's I've connected to. It has made a huge difference to have others show their own insights, caring and curiosity.

Bless you all for connecting with me. You each have truly shown me the light of love in your dedication to your work and through that, your ability to be my co-discoverer, my friend, my student, and my teacher.

You have all been my mentors.

Contents

Introduction I

Chapter 1 ..... Breaking Open .... Page 1

Chapter 2 .... Little Things Matter .... Page 4

Chapter 3 .... The Mind's Eye Views A Crime .... Page 11

Chapter 4 ..... No Preconceptions is Beginner's Luck .... Page 29

Chapter 5 .... Where Are My Children? .... Page 33

Chapter 6 ..... Rachel .... Page 45

Chapter 7 .... A Vision of Murder .... Page 60

Chapter 8 .... Murder Close to Home .... Page 67

Chapter 9 .... Serial Killer .... Page 72

Chapter 10 ... Unsolved Murder .... Page 82

Chapter 11 .... Is He a Serial Killer? .... Page 91

Chapter 12 .... No Answers .... Page 97

Chapter 13 .... Bunny's Stolen .... Page 102

Chapter 14 .... Thoughts on Being a Psychic Detective .... Page 107

Resources .... Page 111

INTRODUCTION

While this is a book about criminal cases, it is also about discovering how we can all make a difference. All life is a creation, a continuous dream, and an exploration that has infinite possibilities. Discovering the endless inner terrain is to glimpse an unending existence. Becoming interested in the mysteries of human nature is not unusual; having the opportunity to apply intuitive powers to uncover hidden truths is, perhaps, less commonplace. Aren't most great law enforcement officers using some of their inner senses? If you know someone in law enforcement, then you know that the best of them are psychic! Maybe the term is not a comfortable one to kick around at a police station or an FBI investigation, yet that's exactly what is being used in all but a few cases.

Intuition is that gut feeling, the hunch, the light bulb going on. It is also a conglomeration of life experience, insight, and a mental antenna focused on the truth. Just like the fine arts, the psychic senses come in a variety of textures and forms. When someone asks if I'm a medium, I hesitate only because I'm torn between explaining that anyone can do all; psychic, medium, psychic healing, intuitive medical work, psychic detective work, animal communication, and so on—or just saying yes. As a psychic detective, I have touched both sides, the deceased victim and the perpetrator. Now, if a soul inhabits a life form or it has shed its form, it should not matter. The energy of all life is interconnected, therefore always available.

To all the victims, their families, friends, community, and law enforcement officers I have worked with, thank you for letting me into your lives and into your pain so that some may find peace. I hope I've helped each and every one of you ease the journey here and beyond our physical lives. May our Creator always be with you.

Two of the best reads (out of print, still available) to help you on this journey are *Witness from Beyond,* conversations between the decesaed theologian A. O. Mattson and distinguished clairvoyant Margraret Flavell Tweddell (my mentor) as edited by Ruth Mattson Taylor, and *On Death and Dying* by Elisabeth Kubler-Ross. Ms. Kubler-Ross remarked that the book edited by Ms. Taylor is "an important book to help in the understanding of life and the transition we call death—which is not the end of life but a new beginning with continued growth and challenges."

Kubler-Ross was a psychiatrist, a pioneer in near-death studies, the pioneer in hospice care, and the author of the aforementioned groundbreaking book *On Death and Dying*.

Medium and former Navy Commander Suzanne Giesemann adds other valuable books on relating beyond the veil. One of her books *Still Right Here* is a remarkable expedition from her previous work to her current calling. I credit two very special women for introducing me to Suzanne's work—Judith Hancox, LCSW, BCETS, and Irene Vouvilades, Judith's sister.
I'm blessed that Judith is my closest female friend. Judith's sister Irene's daughter, Carly, speaks to us from beyond the veil. It was Carly who brought us all together to carry on the work she started. Determined to help those less fortunate, she came through to me shortly after leaving this earth to continue her mission. *http://www.carlyskidsfoundation.com/* was created through Carly's, and her mother's love. Irene is so inspired by her daughter's continuing mission that she now sits on the board of Helping Parents Heal, (*https://www.helpingparentsheal.org/*). This is a beautifully spiritual gathering of parents whose children have left this earth. All are invited to join a local online and/or in-person group.
For all those suffering from the after effects of knowing what harm some humans may create, I offer some ideas on my website and through online classes promoted there, and on my personal Facebook page, (*Nancy Orlen Weber*) and her Instagram *@nancyweber372* to help you sleep better, and live with the knowledge of loss, and find some peace. All the resources mentioned here can be found under Resources at the book's end. .

Out of my need to see more good people embrace the work, I started mentoring both novice and advanced psychics, mediums, and so forth. It is uplifting to find people like Frank Johnson (see my website under mentoring), who is a nurse/psychic and so much more, and so many others who not only have the passion for doing the work but they also have the heart and soul to handle it.

In this bookI've selected some of the criminal cases I've worked, which are followed by exercises that can assist in your search for the truth and, perhaps, open more doors of perception.

If it is in The Plan, then the following ideas may also help guide you to answers you have long sought. It is not enough to say, "I care what happens to others." Action toward serving keeps the gifts growing. I remember the first time I stepped outside my comfort zone and helped when I was asked.

Now I need to create a ripple effect that might inspire others to help. That's where this book and my mentoring program come in.

I'm hoping you take your own gifts seriously.

Give your ability time to develop, to send out the "I'm ready to help" magnetic wave into the universal humanitarian pool. You don't have to work with law enforcement. You can use the exercises even while sitting quietly at home. We all participate with our thoughts, our feelings, and our beliefs. Intention matters. Make yours count.

https://nancyorlenweber.com/mentoring/

"A mentor is someone who allows you to see the hope inside yourself." —Oprah Winfrey.

Chapter 1

BREAKING OPEN

His hands were around my neck, and I knew I had minutes to live—at most. At 6'3" he towered over my 5'7" five months pregnant frame. *I'm dying, no breath. Sink, go limp, protect my baby.* Slowly, as I slumped, letting go of everything except my breath, his hands slid off. Assuming he finished the job, he sauntered into the kitchen. Afraid to open my eyes, I stayed on the floor, hoping the monster I had married hadn't injured our baby. I don't know how much time passed before I opened my eyes enough to see him drinking something while standing by the sink. He seemed calm, believing he had just killed me.

Carefully rising, I stood. Motivated by sudden calm resolve I kept moving toward him. He was looking away. As he turned, his eyes widened in disbelief; I kept walking until I was inches from him.

"I suggest you never sleep again. You ever touch me again, and there will be a knife in your heart." I was shocked at my own words, yet knew I meant every one. I walked away, empowered by my anger. I was afraid to consider that I would not be capable of stopping him again. I understood that the only way I could ever physically cause harm would be when I need to defend myself.

It was important that he believe my statement, even when I knew it not to be true. The anger dispelled the fear. I didn't dare fear him or fear for my child. Believing that my fear would only lead to more problems for my child and myself, I kept quiet, inside and out. I had a history of having to be quiet simply because no one would listen or take action when I was molested by my teacher (I was ten), raped as a teen, attacked by a stranger, and more. As Dr. Alice Miller states in the book *Drama of the Gifted Child*, children who have been seriously abused can develop strong antennae for the next moment. I believe that although I've always been psychic, the power became sharper, more focused, and more empowered the moment I stood against being harmed. It was that moment that broke the absorbed belief that I didn't deserve help in a crisis. I became a warrior to help myself and others in need.

It is also why I eventually left behind my nursing career. Wearing a body brace so I could stand without becoming paralyzed, again and again, I finally gave up. As Helen Keller stated, "When one door of happiness closes, another opens; but often we look so long at the closed door that we do not see the one which has been opened for us." I've looked to use all the crazy episodes of violence done to me in my younger years to gain empathy for all of life, to cast out judging others, to draw strong boundaries, not fences, and to work hard to make a difference. #metoo and #peacematters

I hope these stories inspire you to use the exercises and to explore your own abilities as you participate in this wild, sometimes very difficult, sometimes uplifting path we call life. And so, we begin with some of the situations that have taught me to keep serving, and perhaps they will add to your own path of service.

Exercise: Face Front

The less we carry fear as the power that guides our response to anything, the more capable we are of tuning ourselves to inner guidance. We think of it as centering. Some folks meditate; others swim to relax. Centering simply means to me that we clear our worries out for as long as we can and quietly listen to a deeper, quieter voice within.

We may never hear an actual voice; however, words may pop up when we pay attention; words that convey a peaceful tone. Trust yourself to find a way to rebuild that trust. To be able to connect with our souls and with all else, we need to care for ourselves, and help diminish the inner emotional wounds by choosing kinder paths of learning. Deep breathing, yoga, Tai Chi, mediation, music, art, singing, dancing, and therapeutic tools (see Resources in the back of the book) all of these methods are meant to enhance our journey. There are so many choices in today's world. Remember; choose one. Stick with it long enough to know if it is useful. If it does not seem to be a good fit, go on to another.

Be careful to use your intuition and let it lead the way. It's a perfect way to build back your trust in yourself. Remember, have lots of patience.

This first exercise is simply to choose one thing that will improve your well-being. For me, it began with deep belly breaths. Why not start there? The next chapter tells of what happened as I began to take deep breaths.

"I learned that courage was not the absence of fear,
but the triumph over it.
The brave man is not he who does not feel afraid,
but he who conquers that fear."
—Nelson Mandela

Chapter 2

LITTLE THINGS MATTER

My daughter and I stopped by a friend's house to take her and her seven your old daughter to pick up our younger children at preschool. We stepped into a frantic scene.

"Where are my keys? Sorry, I've been searching everywhere. They're gone."

Without a thought for what popped out of my mouth, I suggested, "Did you try the kitchen?"

"No, I never put them there."

The search continued until I said, "I have to pick my son up on time, so could we at least look in the kitchen?"

Stepping into the kitchen, she gave a glance around and was ready to step out. I went over to a corner counter and looked behind a tall jar, and picked up a set of keys. "Are these the ones?" Yes, they were the ones. Yes, she was surprised.

Around the same year a dear friend, Roy Frumkes, a teacher of directing/writing and more at the School of Visual Arts in New York City, called. You may have seen his name as the Writer/Director of the film, *The Substitute* and subsequent films.

"Nance, we're in trouble, a film is missing, and we need it now," Roy's voice was quivering a bit on the phone. "It's an extremely important piece of work for the school. It's a piece of the *Document of the Dead*. Can you look for it?" *Document of the Dead* is a documentary on film director George C. Romero's work as he filmed *Night of the Living Dead.*

"Roy, is there a storage closet with row upon row of film on the second floor, way down the hall?"

"Yes, at the Film Library where I put it. I'm there now."

Having seen me work long enough, Roy knew just to let me hopscotch in my mind. "Okay, someone needs to look through the far right, the very end of the hall, on the top shelf. It's been misnamed," I was checking my vision as I spoke again. "In fact, it's in a different size canister from all the rest. It's tiny. It's there, filed incorrectly."

"Thanks, Nance, I hope you're right. I'll be calling back either thanking you or asking for more."

Minutes later, Roy called, "Nance, can I borrow your mind for a while? There are a few other things I want to find! It was exactly as you saw it. *Document of the Dead* was not named in a tiny canister next to the larger canisters on the top shelf on the last row on the right in the Film Library. When I come out next weekend, dinner's my treat." Every time Roy goes to the Film Library, guys remark on how that was an amazing find.

Then there is my beloved husband. Dick, my sweet soul mate, likes to tell me, "I married you so I could locate where I put things." True to his style, he has lost most things; glasses, keys, money, papers, and so on. He keeps me in psychic shape! Shortly after we married, while working as a patent designer for a semi-conductor company, he wanted to introduce me to his work and the staff. While at the office, he was called away.

"Nancy, the guys will amuse you for five minutes; I've got to see about something," said Dick as he walked away. "If you get an impression of where I put some platinum, I'd really appreciate it."

"What does it look like?" I said as I looked at the chaos of stuff, rows of shelving from floor to ceiling about forty feet long and nothing organized. Looked to me like a group of kids threw things anywhere.

"Big round discs, about six inches in diameter," his back still turned towards his next venture. "There are three."

Immediately I meandered down the hall of chaos. About a third of the way down, I put my right hand into a pile of "junk" and pulled out a clear plastic bag that contained three round disks about six inches in diameter. I called out: "Guys, is this platinum?"

"You found it!" That was Gary, one of the three guys who worked in semi-conductor development with Dick.

Smiling, I walked out. About 15 seconds had passed since Dick left.

He was still visible, walking down the hall. I shouted, "Dick!"

"Do you need something?"

"No, but you do!"

I held up the items. Dick was thrilled. Perhaps, had I known there was about $3,500 (in 1989) worth of platinum, I might not have been so casual about walking over to the shelves. That little bit of pressure could have changed the outcome.

Sometimes it takes quite a while to get the answers. For me, the beauty of the following moments demonstrate the belief in having patience. It was six months before I would move from Flanders, NJ, and I had a stack of mail to drop off at the Post Office. I've always loved the Post Office there; the two women, Kathy and Eileen, ran the front desks. When one of them didn't smile, I knew something wasn't right.

"What's wrong?" I asked.

Kathy responded, "I lost my diamond engagement ring. Can you help? I'm devastated."

"Do you have a blue carpet in your bedroom?" I hoped the vision was correct.

"Yes!"

"Good, then it's not in the garbage or down a drainpipe. It got stuck in the carpet; it fell down beneath something."

The next time I stopped there, Kathy remarked that she couldn't find the ring. I said I was sorry I was wrong.

Several months later, I moved to another town but still kept my box number in Flanders. I went to close it out a few months later, and there was Kathy with a big smile as she greeted me. "Nancy, I'm so glad you came by. I ordered some new carpet for my room and told the guys who were installing it what you said. When they lifted the old carpet, there was the ring, stuck underneath! I'm so grateful. Thank you!" We hugged as I left.

That was an excellent lesson about timing and patience. Twelve years later, a woman I had lost contact with sent me a copy of her new book to the Flanders post office. Kathy, the Flanders Post Office clerk, forwarded it to me! She was probably looking at her beautiful engagement ring as she wrote my address on the yellow label and stuck it over the old one. It was a wonderful thank you. The funny thing is, once people believe you can do it, it helps you to do it. We all work and play better in an atmosphere of trust and respect. Because our psychic abilities are part of the innate package of life, they can easily be muddied with fear and disrespect. The more I respect me, the more I encourage my soul's flow to the surface of my everyday world.

Then there's my eldest daughter Patty (being a stepmother, I get the privilege of sharing the joys, including grandchildren), and her husband, Brian. They were moving from Chicago to New Jersey. Patty had just arrived in New Jersey when she called, "Hi Nancy. How's dad? Could you possibly help? We can't find our tax papers, and they are due in a few days! Brian and I don't know if they are in Chicago or in the boxes or in the garbage or airplane or at Mom's or...oh, we just can't figure it out, and we have to have them now."

"Patty, I see them upstairs in a room painted blue with lots of blue things in it. In Chicago. It's still there. You haven't moved it out of the room. If Brian is in Chicago, tell him not to move another thing out of that room. Take each thing and look carefully at it. When we are nervous or afraid, we literally go blind looking. No one finds anything that way. Tell him to slow down and go on a fun treasure hunt. It won't take him more than ten minutes that way."

All of us being busy, no one mentioned the taxes again. I forgot about it, and they never mentioned it, until we were visiting them in their new home in Connecticut. One of their friends was saying, "This home is haunted; there are ghosts here, I can feel it."

Brian turned to me and asked, "Nancy, are there any ghosts here?"

"I don't see any, nor do I feel any lost souls around. In fact, it feels particularly peaceful here. Lots of loving memories feel present."

Brian smiled, "If Nancy says there are no ghosts, there are no ghosts. I believe her. When our taxes were lost, she took me right to them, despite her being in New Jersey and me in Chicago."

Exercise: Simply Lost

The common thread for each of the lost and found vignettes is the suspension of all thought and allowing for the flow of spontaneous words. As soon as the question was asked, I started responding. You can do that with yourself and others. Lose anything recently? If it is still around, I can guarantee it is somewhere you never normally would put it. Why? You were not in your normal state of mind when you put it down or dropped it. Your mind was completely focused on something else, and your body simply had no signals from you to rely on, so plop it went!

Yes, it means it can be lost in the landfill dump; you put the keys in the bathroom cabinet; those important papers were thrown out as junk mail; you trusted someone who didn't live up to that trust and walked away with it. Before worrying over it, quiet yourself down.

Did you know we are all electromagnetic? Think of EKG's, EEG's, EMG's, tests that demonstrate electrical impulses. Now imagine that your body/mind is a scanning device, constantly recording information from inside itself and outside. Each day, spend a few minutes teaching your mind what you expect it to do!

Example*:* I'm looking for some papers I misplaced or lost. Instead of the usual frantic hunt, sit down and put the concern/fear/worry as far away as possible by focusing on relaxing your body. Do simple breathing exercises and keep doing it until you can truly only focus on your breath. At this point, begin asking questions (inside voice) of yourself as unemotionally as possible. Look for a simple yes or no. Start with questions that are an obvious no. This helps the mind and feelings to read each other clearly. You want your conscious self to fully understand the subtle stirrings from inside your soul. You may know the obvious answer is no, but you now want to "hear" the internal voice of truth touching your conscious mind. Mentally begin asking yourself questions.

Are the papers at someone else's home? Wait to feel the response—let your mental chatter remain faded out, as background noise. "No," says the feeling.

Are the papers I am searching for in the blue car I owned last year? Again, wait. "No," says the feeling.

Did I throw them out? "No," says the feeling.

Are they upstairs? "Yes," says the feeling.

Where? Scrambled message, wrong question. Too much information required, too soon. *The trust isn't there yet.*

Is it in the bathroom? Yes! Huh? But now go look carefully in the small bathroom where you couldn't possibly put those important papers. I mean, go through everything in the stuffed under-cabinet. Pull out the boxes, and...there it is! How did it get there? Now I remember! They were in my hand while I was searching for a pack of gauze because my girlfriend....and so on.

As you test and challenge yourself, make a list of what is missing. For some of us, it is a short list, for others, quite long. Ask friends if they are missing items; be willing to experiment. If you are doing this via email or phone, close your eyes, and if you can, image the item they are telling you about. Notice the context you see it in. You see a bracelet and lots of gray around it, tell your friend. Ask yourself if the gray is solid, soft, wood, furniture, clothing, etc. Remember to ask yourself questions that require a yes or no answer. Let your friend help by answering your questions.

"I see a soft light gray fabric in a dark space. Does that mean anything to you?" You ask despite your thought that you know nothing. Helping subdues fears of being wrong.

"It could be my coat closet; I don't usually wear gray clothing, but I do have a gray raincoat. Should I check there?" Your friend is now curious.

"Can you do that now so we can either continue, or if we're lucky, stop!"

If you do enough of them, you might indeed find missing items. Not everyone does, but it is a good way of teaching your mind to respond to your directions. Every so often, there is someone who does this, and off they go! A regular Sherlock Holmes, where that which appears impossible is easy and obvious. None of us know what hidden skills, strengths, and abilities we have until we bring them to the light. Start exercising your detective skills today and look back in a year. I promise you, keep at it you will discover abilities that will surprise you.

"It always seems impossible until it's done." —*Nelson Mandela.*

Chapter 3

THE MIND'S EYE VIEWS A CRIME

The most frequently asked question I get, whether lecturing, giving workshops, or just socializing, is, "Did you always know you were psychic?" The answer, of course, is yes, and no. You don't know something is different or unique until it is pointed out by someone else.

The second most popular question is how I began working with the police. That question delights me, for in telling the story, I talk about some of the best people I've had the honor to work with and who, over time, became good friends.

Months after we moved to Budd Lake, I met the first female police officer of Mt. Olive, Michele B. She taught karate to children two miles down the road from our house. My son Jesse, then four years of age, signed up. One day Michele approached me after class. An article had been written in the local paper, "Psychic Communicates with Animals." It mentioned a particular instance of my warning some S.P.C.A. agents (friends since I adopted a dog from a shelter) of a potential danger. They were about to visit a home where neighbors believed the owners had shot their own dogs. I warned them that the son would be on the top of the staircase with a shotgun, the one that killed the dogs. I added that the dogs' bodies would be found buried in the backyard. Based on these predictions, the agents took police officers with them. They had to disarm the son, who stood on the top of the staircase with a shotgun. They dug up the buried dogs in the backyard. These poor dogs had been shot. Having read about my work with animals she asked if I would help on a police matter. "We had a rape in town," said Michelle. "Could you pick anything up on it?" This was the first time I was asked by a law officer to do anything. Being shy since birth and an introvert, I have learned that caring to serve puts those awkward feelings aside.

Immediately my thoughts turned into words, "I see a guy with red hair. He's picking up a large rock and hitting her on the head?"

"Would you mind if my superior speaks to you about it?"

I soon learned that the officer in charge would need to give his approval to either confirm or deny. The next week, Michele introduced Chief of Detectives Ross English as her superior. He asked me to repeat what I had told her. Again, no answer; instead he asked, "Can I come to your office tomorrow with my partner?"

The next afternoon, Detective English and Detective Dave sat in my office. I sat in a chair about ten feet from the blue two-seater couch where they sat. Ross was asking me for the third time what I had seen. After I repeated my response, Ross asked, "We have two suspects with red hair; how can we tell which one?"

Without hesitation, I stood up, and limped across the room and back to my seat, sat down, and said, "That one."

"How did you do that? One of them walks just like you did." Dave said with a befuddled look.

"It's easy, I just became him." My smile was really saying, *Thank God I trusted the gift, and it was right.*

Now we became Ross, Dave, and Nancy, looking at cases. That afternoon, they left my office to return later with all the unsolved, still open cases, some decades old. Weeks later, I was informed that the redhead with the limp was interrogated and confessed. Years later, I recall telling Ross it felt like an overwhelming responsibility; what if I was wrong and they were wasting their time?

"We turn to you when there are no leads or too many. Either way, you give us a direction. If you are right, it's incredible. If you are wrong, so what; you've been right so often, and we've gone down many leads that turn out to be wrong. It's never a waste of time."

In the ensuing years, I lectured to court clerks, judges, and law enforcement officers. It helps me understand how they can't possibly know how to trust someone who calls or walks in to help with their clairvoyance. They need some form of credentials, a recommendation from someone they respect. It is almost a catch-22, but not quite.

The few times I had experienced severe anxiety as an adult, a feeling of fluid electricity would run from my lower spine down my legs. It would be such a strong surge that I would feel my legs lose all strength and begin to buckle. Often, when near someone in a lot of pain, I get this strange sensation. It terrifies me, but it also leaves me absolutely certain we are all connected. It's also been, at times, my warning of danger.

Lying in bed one sunny morning and being afraid to face the day was making me angry. I hate being afraid, particularly of something nebulous. Getting angry at my fear usually helps me overcome all the weak and negative feelings. I get a lot done when I'm angry—and I get a lot done when I'm happy, too. I've used anger and laughter as the vehicles to drive my pain away. I get this wondrous high when I'm pulling the pain along the winds of anger. I reach a point where I see how silly I am, crack up laughing at myself, and it's over. But nothing shakes it on this day. That was unusual since I came to love this room's energy. I started to remember the first day I moved into the Budd Lake home; I stared at the wooden floors that had been worn down with angry feet. Scratch marks were everywhere. The walls and ceiling were peeling, only to show plaster beneath the old paint.

The bedroom seemed sad and unloved. It must have tugged at a closed door inside my psyche. A new desire started to spread. I had to help the room. It was the first time I felt a need to help an inanimate object. As I stared, a vision came to me...The walls had a wainscoting midway through, and rectangular portions surrounded by ivory-painted wood. In the interior boxes was a pattern of blue roses and taupe leaves. The exterior was all ivory. The ceiling had the same wallpaper of roses and leaves. How am I ever going to do that? My neck hurt at the thought of it.

On my mission to love the room, I found the perfect pattern in an English wallpaper. Having limited funds, I gulped at the price. Upon use, I discovered its self-pasted back wasn't staying on the wall. The store refunded me half the price and gave me wall paste. I put as much effort and determination into that room as if I were still at Lincoln Hospital, South Bronx, working in the Intensive Care Unit.

That room needed my care, and as stubborn as the walls were, I was their match.

Covering the floor with a textured sand-colored rug was easy. I pointed, paid, and used it. It was worth it; the results were a soothing room to meditate in. Within months, I was inspired to write poetry, and soon music began to take shape in my head. All for the love of a room.

A year after I had done that, two men showed up at our door. Although bearing no striking resemblance to each other, they turned out to be father and son. The father was slim and introspective looking, quiet brown hair, and brow-rimmed glasses that helped quiet brown eyes greet me. "Hello, I'm Mr. Peters, and this is my son. When I was a young boy, I stayed here every summer. My grandfather had the place built for him."

His son, blond, blue-eyed, wide-face, and muscular, joined in. "My father's told me so much about the place."

"I've been wondering about this house. Every room has a different look to it," I said.

"That's because my grandfather traveled all around the world. He originally worked for Burroughs as an engineer. He was one of the designers of the adding machine. He then went and sold the concept to the world. He designed each room to represent a different country he stayed in and loved. I would love to see it again and show my son."

I turned to the father, delighted at the opportunity. "Great, let's start with the master bedroom."

He stepped in and stopped. His quiet demeanor changed rapidly. His slim body turned into a wiry frame of excitement: "It hasn't changed, it's exactly the same. Wallpaper, rug, paint, all the same. How could that be?"

That was an interesting visit.

The bedroom was even more special after that visit. That's why my anxiety, like an antenna that suddenly moved into a corner of my mind, alerted me that something uncomfortable was about to happen. I was on alert. By noon I started to hunt for my kids. Jesse was still in his pajamas playing Dungeons and Dragons, which was his latest craze. "Why do I have to get dressed?" Jesse was still playing. "Get dressed," I said, "We leave in five minutes. It's the third time I've asked you and the last. You can go in your pajamas."

Rebecca must have changed her outfit three times until she got the "right look." My Gemini child. She has an amazing flair for the use of design. Even when she was three years old, she would borrow some of my clothes to complete the fashion statement she wanted to create. She's now the very gracious owner of Shiny Fish Emporium, where her wearable art and things for all ages abound. Now she gets the pleasure of helping others get the "right" look, toys, and more.

Ten minutes later, the three of us were outside. My blue knight awaited us. In 1979 my brand-new Pacer caught fire the week we were to move to New Jersey. Needing money for the move, I fought to get the best deal. It turned out to be better than just saving money. The blue Chevy Caprice Station Wagon only failed to run well twice in its 180,000-mile life. Both times occurred in the driveways of two of my best friends. One knew how to fix it; the other knew how to call a mechanic and pass the time playing Parcheesi. After that, I nicknamed it the Blue Knight.

Now, with Jesse actually dressed and Rebecca looking beautiful as usual, we all stood by the Blue Knight while I took a moment, eyes closed, to encircle our house with a prayer and to see the Light surrounding it. I couldn't see the Light around my bedroom. The image was stuck. Darkness surrounded the back of the house where my bedroom was. I turned to my thirteen-year-old daughter. "Rebecca, honey, could you pretend to paint a beautiful white light all around the house?"

"Sure, Mommy."

She stood still, eyes focused on the house. About two minutes went by when she turned to me with a puzzled expression; "I can almost get white all around the house. From top to bottom, I painted it white." Right arm stretched out, finger aimed toward the left she said, "The bottom left is dark."

"You sure?"

"Yes, mommy, why?"

"Oh, the same thing happened for me. My bedroom is dark." The morning fear poured into me like a gulp of lightning.

"That's okay, sweetheart, you did a great job. Let's go eat with Phyllis."

My smile was one of those "smile for the children" jobs. I know better; children feel the truth. Fear makes me stupid; so does guilt. I wanted my children to have a day away from the problems that we lived with. Life had been scary for them recently. Jesse's dad, Rebecca's stepfather, and I were in the process of tearing down what we had built; a divorce was in the works.

"Are you kids sitting way in the back?"

"Of course we are," giggled Rebecca.

Grateful for the distance between us, I thought about my beloved bedroom. I cruised down the familiar residential section of Caldwell where Phyllis lived. I pulled into the driveway by a white and pale blue Victorian house. Phyllis' black Jaguar was standing in the driveway as we pulled up alongside.

"Hi, sweetheart; look at you, Rebecca, don't you look beautiful."

My girlfriend's long dancer arms hugged Rebecca. Rebecca stood tall with the grace of a young gazelle. Her long, thick auburn hair and sculpted beauty reminded one painter of Botticelli; "he would have loved her." Next came Jesse's turn. As an eight-year-old going through hurts, he managed to pull away and cling at the same time. Every time I looked at him, I prayed that the humor would return to his blue-gray eyes. We were eating when I blurted out, "I'm being robbed!" I was picking up my chopsticks, ready for another mouthful of Ho Fun, when the vision blew across my mind.

"What?" said Phyllis as she looked at my handbag under the table.

"I mean, my house is being robbed, not here. I just saw two men leaving out my bedroom window. It's too late to catch them; they fled. I'll deal with it when I get back." And promptly went back to eating. Relieved of the anxiety that had plagued me all day, I could go back to enjoying myself. I was also comforted by the idea that there are people in the police department of Mt. Olive Township that I can call upon who would understand how I operate. My reverie was broken by Phyllis asking: "Do you want to leave? Why don't you call the police?"

"No, nothing should spoil our fun. This was supposed to be a day off."

All three looked at me. If I was being robbed, I should do something. If it was my imagination, it's bizarre because it comes equipped with details of other people's lives, looks, habits, etc. Being stubborn, or as I like to think, strong-willed, sometimes has its benefits. Phyllis knew it was pointless to argue. We finished lunch and returned to our car in her driveway. She left me with a, "Call me and let me know. Be careful."

As we headed home, I prepared myself mentally to carefully enter the house. I turned to the kids.

"Okay, listen to me. This is important. Do exactly what I ask of you. Just follow behind me, do not touch anything in the house. Even the front door. I think everything is fine inside, but just in case I'm wrong, I need you to hear me and do what I tell you. Okay, time to go in; follow me."

The three of us must have looked like ducks on an outing. I looked with all three eyes. First, the front door. My physical vision showed the door wasn't tampered with. My psychic eye showed no change in energy. I hoped both visions were accurate. Years before I had dated a man named Steve. He worked at one time repossessing cars. He showed me how to pick a lock and how to know when one has been played with. It has come in handy a few times in life. Unfortunately, it was always because someone wanted something. The last time I looked at a lock was in the Bronx in 1968. I lived in an apartment with a boyfriend on the Grand Concourse, Bronx, NY. We went out at 6:30 PM for dinner and arrived back at 8:30 PM. Key ready to go in the lock, I stopped. "Don't touch the lock; someone's paid us a visit."

He stopped, and I showed him the scratch marks. My boyfriend actually had one of those things called hankies. I used it to open the door. We were greeted with a mess. Drawers open, Nikon camera and jewelry were stolen; they had even taken shirts. It was how I learned to trust my feelings, and to get insurance. Now again I believed I was robbed. We continued our column of three into the hall. We walked on our chocolate-colored shag rug that showed every bit of dirt. A big comfortable rug, stained with "I won't bring any more food into the living room" stains. Our beige corduroy couch sat under a window. Only a year old, it looked like it had been there for decades. It, too, had grown roots. Two of our cats, Sweetie Pie and Mu, were sleeping there. "Kids, go join the cats and keep them company. I don't know where the two men went other than my bedroom. Please just sit there until I'm done checking."

"Why?" said my two baby ducks.

"Just sit still for 5 minutes. I'll be right back. No one is here now but us."

Hoping my intuition was correct, I walked through the living room into the hall and stopped. To the left, my bedroom door stood closed. I had left it open. To the right a staircase leads up to the second floor. Ramona was waiting at the top of the steps. Our beautiful mutt had come to us through a local shelter. Badly abused by her previous owner, she had a broken hip that had not been properly repaired, suffered seizures on an almost daily basis, and had the sweetest face. She was part collie, part shepherd, part mystery, and about 45 pounds of shy love. The children adored her. She never hid her fear, barking at every new sound and smell. Now her eyes were as dark as tar. Her tail was swooped down and held tight. She always barked, even at us. She was so scared she was quiet. Slowly she came to me. "Ramona, it's Mommy. It's okay now. No one hurt you, did they?"

"No," a strange voice inside my head answered. Years of working with animals, plus the loss of one very dear cat, have taught me to listen and believe. As I sat holding Ramona, my right hand stayed on top of her head while I stroked her with my left hand. Closing my eyes to see, I was rewarded quickly. Vision and sound internally took over. I believe I was looking out from Ramona's eyes. I had become her for a moment. My palms opened in a gesture of healing. I prayed, "God, I ask to be a channel of light and love for all concerned, especially for Ramona, whose fear is so strong."

I hear sounds coming from my bedroom—Ramona running down the stairs, barking. The bedroom door began to close. Laughing and stroking her beautiful fur, I knew what had happened.

"Ramona, you're incredible. They were afraid of the big angry dog. I'm glad they locked the door. It would have been terrible if they hurt you."

She was quivering, letting her fear out.

"Go to the kids, sweetheart; they'll take care of you."

She turned and marched into the living room, tail a little bit higher; a hint of a wag started as she heard Rebecca's voice calling her. I hate this, hate this, hate this. Why do people like making others afraid?

Wake up, anger, and help me. I'm frozen at the door. Deep breath. Good. Another one. I put my hand on the door. Good. Now I opened it. Two visions jumped up. To my eyes, my bedroom was still a special place. Bed unmade, standard procedure; years of being a nurse cured me of the desire to make beds. Closet doors closed, no dresser drawers open. My body knew differently. Intruders! Call the police. Take a look first and see what happened. It's over, it won't happen again. Oh yeah, that's exactly what I said after someone raped me.

Lying in my bed, an intruder attacked me. He got away, and I was so upset I ran quickly into the first strong arms I found, Dr. Gilbert Arnold Preston. How psychic can you get? Six months later, we married and moved to Puerto Rico, where he showed his other side. Pregnant and almost killed by his hands, I left him as soon as I could, and two years later, we were divorced. I learned that my fear numbs me to the truth.

Back in my beautiful Budd Lake home, I let my eyes relax and began to breathe slowly. I relaxed and asked to be a channel for healing and love. Consciously, I opened my third eye and focused with intent, dropped fear, dropped fury, and went dead calm. Ready, aim, see...the room is in chaos. Jagged waves of light filled the room. Muddy colors scorched the air. At the window, breaking the lock from the outside, stand two young men, one standing on the other's shoulders, both with dark, unkempt hair. Daniel, a young man who once did some sheetrock for us a few years back, was easy to identify; slight of build, pock marked-cheeks, and sloped shoulders. His partner's name, John, was written in my mind. Daniel pries open the window. He jumps into the room and walks over to my jewelry box sitting on the oak dresser. He opens up the doors of the box and takes my new watch, then leans his hand on a wall and one finger rests on the base of a brass lamp as he takes the rare coins meant for my children.

I walked over to my dresser to double-check the vision. Watch— gone. Coins—gone. Okay, Universal Mind, where is it?

Sitting on a dresser in a bedroom at John's girlfriend's apartment in Kings Village.

Daniel walks over to the closet on the left. My husband's closet. He opens the closet door and looks around. He grabs something. It's a rifle. Daniel takes the rifle and runs to the bedroom door. Ramona is barking. I feel his fear. He closes the door and races to the window, hands John the watch and rifle, jumps out the window, and tries to close it behind him. Now they are walking up the back to the path in the woods leading to the Eagle Rock Apartments. Daniel enters an apartment, rifle in hand. He opens the attic door and climbs in with the rifle. He climbs back out empty-handed.

"Okay, kids, you can move. Just don't go into my room."

"Why?"

"Some men came in through the bedroom window and took some of our belongings."

"Why can't we go in?"

"Because that is the only place they went, and the police will look for evidence and fingerprints in that room. We don't want to confuse them. Go anywhere else in the house. Do you know that Ramona kept them from going into the rest of the house? Give the wonder dog extra special hugs."

I walked over to the phone.

"Mt. Olive Police Department," the dispatcher stated.

"I'm reporting a burglary that took place in my home this afternoon while I was out. Please send someone over."

Tables turned; it was my turn for help. With my address and name given to the dispatcher, I hung up and waited. I listened for the sound of our metal lion banging against the huge wooden front door. About five minutes passed before I answered the door. Not recognizing this particular officer, I introduced myself. "Hi, I'm Nancy. Thank you for coming. Let me show you where it occurred."

Ramona was back to normal; she barked non-stop until I asked the children to take her upstairs with them. Out of sight of the scary new person, she would quiet down. The officer and I entered the bedroom. He walked in, and I showed him the window.

"This lock was fine when I left and in place," I said as I looked at the broken lock.

"Hello, where's everybody?" An unmistakable voice leaped across the living room.

"In here, follow the sound of my voice. Hi Dave," I spoke with gratitude for a familiar face.

"You know each other?" The officer asked as Dave brought his full 240-pound bulk into the room. His shock of blond hair and round cherub features softened his 6'1" frame into a non-threatening look.

"Sure, I know Nancy; just let her tell you everything she knows, no matter how odd it sounds. Take it all down, don't leave out anything." Dave was bending over by the window as he continued, "Why didn't you call the department, we would have been right over. I heard it on the radio."

"I didn't want to bother you."

"How were they able to break into your home?" Dave asks.

"I couldn't put light around the bedroom. They must have planned it for days."

Dave just nodded in understanding, the other officer looking more bewildered. "Do you see what happened?" Dave was watching me pace the room.

"Yes, it's coming in pretty clear."

"Okay, start writing what she says," Dave said as he turned to the officer.

The officer had his pad and pen ready for action. Not even a questioning look. I was impressed. He must be curious; I bet he plays poker well. Barefoot and darting from window to dresser, then the brass lamp, then closet as I recounted what I saw.

"Do you have all that?" Dave questioned the cop.

"Yes."

"Do you know what make, what caliber?" The officer was determined to get details.

"Not a chance. I refuse to be able to learn those things. I'll ask my husband when he gets home, and I'll call it in. Ready for more?"

"I think I know these two." Dave looked thoughtful.

"You do? Good, that means I may get back my things. Lose the gun in the evidence room forever, please. I just saw them buying franks with the rare coins; and me a vegetarian. I think that's all I've got." "Did Daniel wear gloves?" That was Dave.

"No, you'll like the print on the brass. It's perfect." That's me. The print stood out. The room became soft hues, quiet while the print looked like it was a bold highlight.

The officer bagged the brass lamp. Dave and the officer left after details of the value of the items were written into the report. By this time, it was 3:00 PM and the theft had occurred at 12:30 PM. Detective Lt. Ross English called me at 7:00 PM to come in. A two-minute drive, and I was there. Requesting to speak to Ross English, the dispatcher buzzed open the door. Ross was reclining, hands over head and a grin that the Cheshire Cat couldn't match as he spoke. "I called Daniel and told him to come here immediately. He came with his mother. I let her stay while I confronted him with the fact that there was an eyewitness."

"Ross, you have to be kidding."

"I got the report from Dave, and we had four search warrants within the hour from the judge. You were an eyewitness to it. It's not trickery. I just wanted to see what he had to say. He denied it at first. He confessed when I told him the gun was in the attic. At that point, he confessed to everything. Told me he climbed in the window, took your watch, coins, and gun, and got out before the dog could tear him apart.

"He didn't ask how anyone could see him go into his mother's attic. When I told him that the eyewitness saw him do it, he and his mother took Dave and me to their apartment. Using one of the search warrants, we retrieved the gun."

"But didn't he question how someone could see into the attic?"

"Not for a second. I sound like I know it's a fact; they believe me. To go on, Dave then took another officer and went to John's girlfriend's apartment in Kings Village. When they got to the door, she stood there telling them they couldn't come in without a search warrant.

They handed her the warrant and went in. Dave went right over to her bedroom dresser and picked up your watch, told her she was in trouble for receiving stolen property and left. By the time he returned here (the apartments were both less than five minutes from the police station), we received a call from John. He was at a phone booth near the Dairy Queen, begging us not to shoot him. He confessed on the phone and asked if he could please come in. That's about eight hours from start to finish. That's what happens when you have an eyewitness who sees clearly."

"Ross you are hysterical."

We continued to celebrate with smiles and good feelings. I hoped that these young men would reconsider the path they embarked on. Ross told me this was not the first crime they committed. I hoped it scared them enough for it to be their last. Days later, Ross told me it was the talk of the station. Everybody was amazed, and confusion was afloat. That may be why everyone there became very hospitable when I would visit. Ross and Dave supported the idea that police have a right, when they question suspects, to say that they were seen or they have latent fingerprints to trick people into saying they did it. Not lying, just getting them to tell the truth. There is no reason to admit it if they think you have nothing on them. And, after they obtained the confessions, the fingerprint on the lamp, nice and clean, proved the case as well. Both men eventually were given a jail sentence, which they served.

During a crisis, it is almost impossible (there may be one capable person on this planet) to stay objective and calm; unless that is your innate style. Most of us are a mixed bag; some are calm helping others and freak out afterward, some are immobilized by fear, others are hysterical, and so on. The spectrum of behavior is wide. Had I not started to breathe deeply and consider a universal point of view years before this incident, I doubt if I would have been of any assistance to myself, my children, or the police. I hold a strong belief that it was also given to me to know because it would serve as an opportunity for these two young men to reconsider their lives. Who knows who else they might encounter?

Retired Chief Detective Ross English recalled something that we were quiet about for years.

"An amazing incident that the entire force still talked about for years is when Nancy called me saying, "I need to speak with you in person. It cannot be over the phone." This was about a couple of hours after we found a bug in the captain's office. We were keeping it a secret; concerned about the significance of the bug. She had no way of finding out except through her powers. I came over with the troops. The chief and the rest of the top guys. We brought over a bunch of photos of all the cops, and Nancy picked out Giella right away. She said he is going to be very serious trouble; he is trouble, there is something strange going on. She even said he should be under suspicion for planting the bug. She believed he was stealing evidence out of the evidence room and selling guns illegally. She was upset and told us he would blow up the town if he could."

"She also pointed out a guy named Donnie. She thought he was a possible arsonist. Donnie's house had burnt down that year, but they found nothing conclusive. We, the police, found the bug and knew it was from Radio Shack but there were so many stores; I was exhausted from seeking. Nancy held up the bug and stated the date of purchase and the store from which it had been purchased. We went the next day, and there was the receipt for that particular bug on the exact date Nancy told us, September 11. It was made out to a guy she traced as working for another town. The chief was so impressed he asked Nancy to be an auxiliary officer and gave her a badge. Interestingly, the guy who purchased the bug lived in the same town as Giella, and he could have purchased it for him."

"Within the year, Nancy was asked to return her badge, and I was demoted, along with another officer. The chief was under investigation for theft from the attorney general's office. He believed that Nancy, another officer, and me had known of his criminal activities through Nancy's gifts. He was forced to resign. There were two other young guys who worked with Giella and left. The county prosecutor got in touch with me because they felt I was the only credible person in the department whom they could trust for internal investigations. They introduced me to the sergeant in charge of their official corruption unit. They had a suspicion that something was going on with Giella. They had someone who saw him take pieces of a gun in the evidence room and put them in a paper bag, and (presumably) take it home. The prosecutor's office was after Giella because of a previous incident where he was charged in a bribery case. They went to a jury trial, and Giella won it. The prosecutor felt he was still dirty and had to be eliminated as a policeman. I was introduced with a Detective Jones (not a real name) and the prosecutor's office told our interim chief that I was to work with Jones in regard to some other problems in the department. Then I was told that the new chief wasn't to be trusted. He was eventually removed, and I was put back in as a detective. At that point, Giella was the target. There was now a new acting chief, and I was also assigned to work with a federal agent from the ATF (Alcohol, Tobacco, and Firearms) on Giella."

"Before the raid of his house, Jones and I conducted an investigation. I wore two body tapes; we did an inventory of the evidence room. We found many parts and guns missing. It was to the point that Giella was under total suspicion. Then I had Giella do an inventory with me. When I asked him to show me certain weapons and he wouldn't, I said

'Hold it up. That's just a skeleton of it; where's the rest of it?' He said, 'I don't know.' So, I asked, 'What happened to these?' And Giella says, 'I don't know.' I said, 'You and I are the only two who have keys to it, and you're the evidence custodian. As far as I'm concerned, I didn't take them. Where the hell are they?' His answer was, 'I don't know.' At that point, the prosecutor's office walked in, identified themselves, read him his rights, and let him call his lawyer."

"He was taken to his house, and a search warrant was executed. Well, the investigation went on from there. That's when I called Nancy and informed her that everything she said was coming true. She then told me there were barrels of explosives. We got another search warrant and went back in and found the explosive powder! He was allowed to have some because he made reloads. A factory load of a 38 or 357 bullet or a 45, after it's fired, can be reloaded by putting a new primer in, filling it with gun powder, and putting a wadcutter in. It's different from the actual factory bullet. It's a piece of lead, and they're used in practice. He had more explosive than he was allowed. He was indicted. He then turned state's evidence against many, which led to many arrests. They were satisfied that he had earned his non-prison custodial sentence. He had pleaded guilty to one count of official misconduct; we had 152 counts against him. He was sentenced to five years in jail and a ten thousand dollar fine. The five years were suspended. He moved his family out of the state, paid the fine, and flew out himself that very same day to join them."

"Jones became the new chief. He was called by ATF and told Giella was arrested for possession of explosives, stolen, I believe, from a National Guard armory. He was in the process of selling them to mercenaries. Giella was mum about official misconduct on record from Mt. Olive Township. Chief Jones and I volunteered to go down to the state where Giella was living and fill them in. That became unnecessary when Giella learned that we would. He is now serving many years in prison in another state."

Exercise: Details, Details, Details, Get Used to Them.

The first year I was giving classes, I studiously kept notes on all the connections I attempted to make, even with situations broadcast over the radio. One day I heard a radio report that a school bus of children and their driver were missing. The report came from California. Staying with the promise I made to practice what I taught, I sat quietly, hands relaxed on my lap, palms upward, eyes closed, and asked the Universal Source of Life (insert the name/words that you use) to "use me as a healing instrument in the situation with the school bus in California." I kept repeating this until I felt it was an all-encompassing thought. Nothing else mattered. Whether my imagination was more vivid or I was tuning in, I did not know. Nor did I care. I needed to feel helpful. The movie in my mind started.

I see a kind, short, stocky, bus driver with brown hair and shoes, handing children sandwiches, comforting them by promising he would lead them to safety. A bus inside a rock quarry 30 miles from the start point continues the vision. Three people moving around. Two men with huge automatic weapons and a woman with dark braided hair. The woman seems apart from the action, just there. A message comes:, "They will be led to safety by the bus driver, who is a wonderfully heroic man. They will be safe and unharmed."

I wrote this all down, date and time included. Turning on the radio again, I heard that the police believed the bus driver had kidnaped the children. I called the police in California, who promptly dismissed me. How could they possibly know that I "saw" something?

How did I know I was right? I didn't. The next report was that they were all discovered and safe. My vision was confirmed; the bus driver fed them and led them to safety, away from a rock quarry 30 miles from where they were first taken. The two men were captured. The woman was and still is the mystery. One child claimed to see a woman with dark braided hair. No one else did. I thought about it as I braided my dark brown hair, wondering what is real and what is imagination.

No, I didn't help the police with that situation, and I didn't hop on any plane or drive somewhere. I stayed home, and yet I believe I helped. We have all seen what group energy can do; now, look deeper and see what group energy of compassionate and loving thoughts can do. Each of us adds to the thought fields that are shared by all.

There is an ancient Hebrew saying I once heard, "Only the broken heart is an open heart." We all understand that some of our ability to empathize and have compassion comes from our painful and sometimes tragic stories. Our helplessness also comes from our past, usually from our childhood and sometimes from being at the receiving end of abuse at any age. Consider that these situations can be the springboard to our own powerful wings opening wider and taking us to previously unimagined heights. When we work first on facing our own pain and anger, we release feelings that fear suppressed. Once clarity emerges, you may feel frustrated in not knowing where and how to direct the energy that surfaces from the conscious awareness of the suffering we have endured. To amplify this powerful trauma recovery awareness, power up your empathy and compassion and, exercising discernment, reach out to others in their own emotional pain. Two of the best resources I've found for offering recovery aid are specific essential oils and special music. These tools can create a gentle, peaceful, and clear state of consciousness. For specifics on such help with trauma recovery and general self-help, please refer to the Resources in the back of this book.

"I think we all have empathy. We may not have enough courage to display it." – Maya Angelou

Chapter 4

NO PRECONCEPTION IS BEGINNER'S LUCK

There were about eight students gathered for my Thursday night Psychic Development Class. It was in its third year. I never knew who would show up. I feel there are enough horrible surprises, so I like to balance them out with fun, happy surprises. We began a guided meditation, and I noticed everyone was fidgeting. I threw out a question about healing. We did some exercises, and then someone mentioned that he couldn't get the Son of Sam case out of his mind. That explained the disquieting energy of the group that night.

I commented: "Want to do something about it?"

We all joined hands while seated in a circle. I started by praying, "Dear Creator of All Life, thank you for our moments on earth. Our gratitude is unending. We seek to be Channels of Your Love, Your Light. We offer our energies in whatever way you deem is spiritual in the matter of Son of Sam. We ask that if it is spiritually appropriate, stop him from destroying others. Put him where he can be of no further harm." A few moments of silence followed. I continued, "Now, everyone, let go of each other and place your hands on your laps, palms facing upwards. Send your Universal Healing Energies to the Son of Sam situation; to the victims, their families, the people helping, and all others involved. Visualize or feel the energies as Universal Light flowing through you and out through your hands."

After the exercise, everyone took a turn and told what their experience was. I wrote it all down, including the date and time. Each person shared their vision/thought/feeling. We went around in a circle.

"It was awful; all I could feel was the horror," the person to my right said.

The next one said, "Just saw darkness; was too afraid to come closer" And so on, until Barbara...

"I saw a young man, very white skin, dark hair, and his name was David Berkowitz. That's all I got."

And the next person spoke, "Horrible, blood, anger. Left me hurting."

This continued until my turn...

"I also saw a young man, similar coloring to Barbara's, and his name was Richard David Falco."

"That's incredible! That must be his name. Call the editor of the Post. You know, the one who Son of Sam is writing to," said one of the students immediately after I spoke.

"Just because I'm the teacher doesn't make me any more accurate than Barbara, or anyone else. Let's send the editor, in writing, both names. Since it is getting late, I'll send it tomorrow."

Tomorrow came, but there was no need to send the letter. The morning news told of David Berkowitz's apprehension through a motor vehicle ticket. Two weeks later, stories about his life were in every paper. They included the fact that he was adopted and that his birth certificate name was Richard David Falco. That was the second class Barbara had ever attended. She was just beginning her new journey of listening inside.

Assume nothing. If you want to make a difference, find others who also care. There is strength in numbers. You don't even have to physically meet; just work together toward the common good. Keep notes, and record what comes through you while quietly focusing on a situation. It's a good idea to stay away from details in a situation. Just look and listen to headlines. If you are going for accuracy and care to make a difference, you want to be able to know what you are picking up versus what you heard or read. When working on a criminal case, I usually tell the first person to contact me, "Please do not tell me anything other than the nature of the crime...rape, murder, etc. It doesn't help me to know more; I can end up making rational assumptions instead of listening to my soul."

Do not be afraid to be wrong. It's important to accept mistakes. If you don't, you will eventually be trapped by your need for power, your need to be more important than anyone else in the situation. Be glad you are human.

Criminal cases are extremely challenging on all levels. After working on these situations, it becomes easy to work with issues involving everyday kinds of problems. Perhaps if we all meditated and prayed for all situations, from a mugging down the street to a major war, we could see the magical powers of our Creator pouring peace and love everywhere. We are part of the problem when we stand aside watching in a "do nothing" posture.

Exercise: Soul Consideration

Pick up a newspaper, read online, turn on a radio or watch a TV news report. When you get to some news that throws you off-center, something that stirs your emotions, put the paper down or turn off the news. Sit quietly and focus on restoring your breathing pattern and letting go of all tension. Once you are sufficiently back in your body, not letting your mind jump you into fragments, open yourself up as a conduit for the healing light. First, let it cleanse and restore you, freeing you first of fears of the jagged edges of life. Only after you are sufficiently calm and feeling the universal spirit embrace you, open your mind, your heart, and being to sharing the Light and Love of the Universal Divine Presence with the disturbing situation. Keep the critic, the judge, and the authoritarian opinions for later; it doesn't help. Strong opinions and strong emotions are part of the chemistry that dilutes the power to perceive accurately. Remember to send it to the whole situation, then to the individuals you may be concerned about.

Gloria Estefen was recovering beautifully from her broken back when she stated to the press that she could feel the love and prayers sent to her from the very beginning. She went on to say she believed that this was the impetus for her recovery, the support she needed to find her way back. No one can do it all alone; we are all connected whether we want to be or not. Once we join in lovingly, the message we send out is clear, and the universe can respond in kind.

Each day of your Soul Life, take a few minutes to be grateful for your existence; extend this loving gratitude towards the existence of all your family and friends (regardless of what you think of them).

Keep extending your love and gratitude towards others. Include animals, insects, plants, soil, rocks, etc. Spiral this feeling towards a larger and larger community until you feel your connection to all, even beyond this planet.

Now you are taking a strong stand for Creation. Applying this attitude at the beginning of your day helps reinforce a spiritual direction. Do this often, daily if possible. A belief system that accepts all life as holy creates an immense cleansing of all fear-based beliefs. For the last fifteen years, each morning, I anoint myself with amazing essential oils (check the resources in the back of the book). The frequency of these oils harmonizes perfectly with my spiritual intention. It becomes much easier for me to maintain a balance between what I've seen of the dark side of our species and the amazing, glorious divine spark of humanity in many. It's worth the effort!

"Our sorrows and wounds are healed only when we touch them with compassion." – Buddha.

Chapter 5

WHERE ARE MY CHILDREN?

It was the early 1980's, and I had just returned home from a local radio talk show when the producer called. "Hi, Nancy, this is Glen from WMTR. We just got a call from a woman who said her grandchildren were abducted, and she wanted your number. Can we give it to her?"

"Absolutely."

The phone rang within five minutes. A wobbly voice spoke, "Hello, I'm Mrs. Keyes. I heard you a little while ago, and I thought maybe you could help my daughter. Her children were stolen by her ex-husband, and she has no idea where they are. It's been five months."

"Mrs. Keyes, I'm so sorry for your troubles. I don't know what I can do. All I can do is attempt to help. I never know beforehand what I will be capable of. Each case and every situation is so different. Why don't you have your daughter call me? Does she live in New Jersey?"

"Yes."

"Do you think she can come to my office in my home? I think it would be easier for us in person."

"Can she call you tonight?"

"Sure, just tell her I finish work at about 8:00 PM tonight. Any time after that and before 10:00 PM."

We rang off, and years of discipline began kicking in. Every day, I thank the teachers at Brooklyn College School of Nursing and my early years of training. They keep paying off. I didn't want to second guess the events I was about to get involved in, so I moved my mind and body into a routine of work.

8:30 PM... "Hello, my mother called you today. I'm Jillian."

"Oh, yes, hi Jillian. Your mother told me your children were taken by your ex-husband. Please don't fill me in right now. There will be plenty of time to tell me what you know after I look into it my way. Do you have photos of your children, and can you come to my home office in Budd Lake?"

"Yes, I can, and I'll bring the photos. Anything else I need to bring?"

"Just an open mind. I really don't think I need anything else to start with. You know I can't promise you results. I'll have a tape recorder (early 1980's) going, and you will keep the tape we make. Sometimes, things come to me in pieces like a jigsaw puzzle, and we have to figure it out afterward. I never know beforehand how things will go."

"How much do you charge?"

"Jillian, by the time it's over, you will be deep in debt from your search. I'm not about to add to your burdens. There will be no charge for any of my services. Feel free to use me and call on me as needed."

We hung up, and my mind tried to go numb, but my heart wouldn't let it. How could I charge her? I could be next. My daughter's father was suing me for custody, his threats of abduction not far from my mind. He'd tried to snatch my daughter just to hurt me. Jillian's story was far too close for comfort. Everyone who studies metaphysics marvels at the synchronicity that occurs as we stay in the flow of the life force. It is not unusual to have people walk into our lives holding up a mirror to our own. For the next few days, I was afraid to let my children out of my sight. Normally they could run around in the mall, visit friends and, in general, have a lot of freedom. These days were different. The fear was so strong I could hear the beat of my heart day and night. My eyes were commanded to stay frozen on my children. Don't let them out of sight for a second. I was running on empty, exhausted, and terrified. The psychic side, or as I think it, my soul sensing, was not allowed its usual place in my life.

Five evenings after the call, Jillian arrived. The sweetest face had the saddest smile. Her dimples couldn't hide the pain. Her eyes were in a constant state of terror; large pale blue freaked out eyes. Jillian handed me a picture of her three children standing with her ex-husband, Joe. Because there were no centralized computers, no

Missing and Exploited Children's Bureau, and a distinct lack of protective laws, Jillian was limited in what she could do. Parental abductions in 1980 were considered between the parents and a misdemeanor at best. Jillian told me that her former husband, Joe, had been living in the family home with their three children: Diane, seven, Jean, six, and John, three. They had a custody trial in June of 1980 in which Jillian was awarded custody of the children and the house. The judge granted Joe one more week with the children, after which he was to vacate, and she would move back in with them. After six days, Joe disappeared with the children.

The first and most immediate impression, while I held the photograph, was that the children would come home. For me, that is unusual. I'm generally careful not to hold out hope or fear, just to look into the now. I also felt it would take a long time before that could happen. When a psychic looks at time, it's different than when we are in the normal thinking mode. What is a long time? I ask myself questions constantly. You need to teach your own subconscious what you want and give yourself permission to know things. Just keep the Universal Laws in mind; don't say anything that could harm, but if it is yours to say hard and direct things, give it gently and lovingly and help the other person through. Being psychic is not enough; how we use it is, I believe, far more important than having it. Honesty can be brutal or gracious; choose to be gracious where possible.

Looking again at the photo, I suddenly had an image of the state of Texas. Jillian was excited. There were indications that Texas could be a location. Our meeting came to an end, and as I led her to the door, Jillian asked, "Can I bring the sheriff's investigator back with me?"

We set a date, and Jillian arrived with County Sheriff's Investigator, Lou Masterbone. Lou was obviously skeptical and yet was willing to do whatever was needed to help Jillian recover her children. There are two magic ingredients in Lou's soul; the first, loyalty to his friendships. He had known Jillian in high school and became actively involved in the case out of his desire to help a friend. The second piece of magic is his own desire to help children through any problem. Long before the tragedy of missing children was commonly known and before police were required to investigate parental abductions, Lou studied with an expert on missing children and adults, Dick Rufino. Dick Rufino was a member of the Sheriff's Department in Bergen County, NJ. When you hear that name, give a moment of thanks. If it wasn't for this one man's passionate concern for all missing people, Adam Walsh's father would not have been as capable of taking steps without Dick Rufino to create the 501(C3), the National Center for Missing and Exploited Children®. Dick inspired countless law enforcement agents to care. While Dick Rufino is no longer a participant on this planet, his work still lives on in every person who dedicates themselves to helping. If he is listening from the other side, I hope he understands my need to give him credit. I have a two-hour recording of the only interview he agreed to give on his expertise in working with missing people. A humble man, he refused all offers for television, magazines, and more. He stayed on this earth to benefit all until he was called home.

As I took them to my office on the second floor of my home, Lou was telling me, "I called two other police officers, Bill Hughes, and Ross English, for references. They said they worked with you and told me you were good. I just want you to know I still do not believe in all of this. I'm only here because Jillian needs support."

Because of the serious nature of the issue involved, it was easy to put aside my ego's need not to be rejected. As a result, my insecurities didn't come storming out. That would have been tragic. We worked about three hours that night. The first thing I saw in my mind was the map of Texas and I felt a connection between the map, the children, and Joe. I got an encyclopedia and turned to the map of Texas, looking for one place on it to stand out, much like bold, italicized words. Sometimes it simply feels like my attention is drawn to that, whatever that is, like a magnet pulling on me. There it was... "Euless, Texas," I felt energized when I spoke, as if I finally let go of something.

Lou said, "We know he's been there. We tracked him originally through the children's school records to Euless, Texas. Unfortunately, by the time we tracked him, he had already left. We have no idea where he is at this point."

I went on: "Jillian, I see Joe telling your children that the devil has you, that you were taken away to a mental hospital. They don't know what to believe, but your eldest knows you are not mentally sick. She doesn't believe him; she is just too young to be independent enough to call the police. She is also afraid of the consequences. They are being fed, housed, and clothed, although not with the kindness and consideration you have given them. Their clothes and shoes are too tight. Most of his actions are done to spite you."

Throughout the evening, we would drift away from the intensity and just go over what I had already stated, hoping to see something else I missed. Each time we went over it, another little piece of information would pop out. It was as if I kept rerunning the movie and each time would be able to recover another piece of the film. I finally had something else, "He left with a woman who is still with him. His friend gave him a truck. He's become a very religious person, more fearful fanatic than a true believer. Fanaticism is terror turned outward. He can't be questioned; he's rigid. I see him having beaten you when you two were together. Is that true?" The images were not in a neat sequence.

"Yes, he was violent at times."

"Please do not fear that for the children. He has never been violent towards them, has he?"

"No."

"I do not see him ever being violent with them. Totally inappropriate, yes. He was violent with you in front of them. That's why your eldest would hesitate to reach out to anyone. She's not sure how he would treat her. He's making her do some of the household responsibilities. How old is she? I see her as about seven years old."

"Yes."

"Your younger daughter will have a few stitches right above her upper lip, but it is not through his actions. Please do not get scared. He didn't do it. It's a dog bite; the dog is not rabid, she is okay, and he is very solicitous of her with this incident. She will recover nicely."

It always seems that once there is a glimpse into someone's life and I go back to it, other parts of the tapestry of who they are and what happens in their life simply present themselves. The term Direct

Knowledge, metaphysically speaking, simply means we don't see it, hear it, smell it, taste it or touch it mentally; it's just there. I caught a mental glimpse that felt associated with the children, "I see snow on the mountains, but it is warm where they are."

Ever try and remember something and the harder you try, the further away it seems to get? Memory, including psychic pick up from someone else, is no different. Peripheral vision is best. Drop it, leave it alone, get your mind and brain busy on something else, and it will pop up! Towards the end of the first hour, Ramona, our sweet dog, meandered in and plopped down over my feet, promptly going to sleep. Having helped ward off burglars, Ramona was royalty. Continuing our talk, Lou Masterbone asked, "Do you see where they went after Euless, Texas?"

Me: "'E' Street in California. It's not too far from the ocean; I can smell it."

"What town?" Lou asked.

"Can't see it. Can see the dirt road. Feel the warmth. Don't know even if it is north or south, no clue yet, just keep talking."

"I need to know the town; California is a big state," Lou insisted.

"I know, but asking me again won't get it. We need to move onto something else, and then, hopefully, it'll come."

"Okay, is he still with the woman you saw?"

"Yes. He'll marry her. She knows the children are being told lies. I don't get it. She seems nice, but she's got to be trouble to go along with him. I see checks his mother wrote to him. The canceled checks are lying on her desk. They are the key to finding him. You know what's weird? His mother will turn them over to the court if asked."

"No, she wouldn't do that," Lou commented.

"Yes, she will. She'd be afraid not to."

The night wore on, and I wore out. We made another appointment to get together in my office, and as soon as they left, I went promptly to sleep. At the next appointment, Ramona joined us again, lying across my feet. We continued in the same manner, going over most of what we had said before. Lou kept asking what town I saw them in California. For the fifth time, Lou asked, "What town in California, I need to know." Ramona woke up and looked at me. Thinking she needed me, I said, "Ramona?" I looked at her, looked at Lou, and wham, "Ramona, California." I had no idea if that was any place at all. I just wanted to end the conversation.

"Ramona, California? Okay, now we can go with that," Lou seemed pleased as he spoke, while I wondered if Ramona, California existed.

Apparently, Lou gave some information to the lawyer because Joe's mother had to go for depositions and was told she had to bring her bank account with her. Strangely enough, she did. She gave Jillian's lawyer all the things she had pertaining to her account. Of course, there was no address on Joe's checks except the bank's stamped on the back. It was a San Diego bank.

Turns out there is a Ramona, California, and it is in San Diego County. Days later, Jillian called. "He's there, Nancy; he's on E Street in Ramona, California. Lou is calling the San Diego Police Department to investigate. He asked them to go. I hope they check on him soon."

Because the laws did not see parental abduction as a felony in 1980, most law enforcement agencies did not get involved for the first several months of this case. Out-of-state courts would not enforce custody without legal representation and the presence of the accusing parent. All of this took months, chunks out of Jillian's life. Now it felt like it was coming closer to the end. By this time in the search, President Carter had signed the bill making parental abduction an indictable offense, however, it had not been tested yet. Jillian was calling regularly, checking in, seeing if I had anything new to offer. Then one day, "Nancy, Lou just called; the San Diego police finally agreed to check on them tomorrow. Nancy, will I see my children this week?" Jillian anxiously asked.

"I don't see it, Jillian. I don't know why, but there will be a delay. You will see them within the next few weeks. And Jillian, they will all remember you."

After months of waiting, tomorrow would be too late. Everything inside me wanted to shout at the police, "Go now!" Here's where faith, belief, and acceptance that none of us control anyone else comes into play. Staying peaceful in moments like these is a full-time job, and most of the time, I'm not capable unless the faith in Divine Wisdom takes over. The call came in from Lou, "The police found the apartment empty. He and the kids moved the day before. But we're lucky; he told a neighbor where he was moving. Hawaii, to the big island. I'm going to the judge and asking for a warrant to extradite him back to New Jersey. With luck, the Hawaiian police will arrest him. It's a strange case. We're always one step behind Joe and the kids. Every time we get to where we track them, they're gone."

Lou told me later that when the judge asked him, "On what grounds are you requesting this"? Lou told him he was working with a psychic and trusted her information. The judge granted the warrant. This was the first test case in New Jersey on child abduction by a parent. Many years later, I was walking in a town where the judge lived. He was retired and was sitting on his porch. He recognized me and we chatted for a moment. I asked, "Why did you agree to the bench warrant when Lou told you it was a psychic?" He said that issuing a bench warrant on something untested was a unique and somewhat perilous task for a judge. He knew Lou to be a very practical and good investigator. "If he vouched for you, that was sufficient for me."

"This time is different. He won't move." Lou hung up and continued the long journey of fourteen months working on finding these children.

Two days later, "Nancy, it's Jillian. Lou got the warrant from Judge Gold. He told them a psychic informed him! The judge said if you believe her, I do too. We're hoping the Hawaiian Police won't question the warrant. You know this is testing the new law. I'm so scared, and I don't have the money to go yet. I have to wait a week. My lawyer has to go too. They tell me it's the only way to be assured the law will help."

"This time, he's not running. The children are too much for him, but he can't own up to what he's done." I was feeling happier by the moment. The belief that this was true was flooding me with relief.

"He needs to be caught, and his soul knows that. He's staying right where he is."

The next week, Jillian called, "I've got the ticket to Hawaii and one for my lawyer; do you think we're near the end?"

"This is it, Jillian; you will see your children on Friday at 4:00 PM sharp. They will walk under an arch with a clock right above."

"Seriously, you think it's over?"

"Jillian, I am as sure as I can be the way I do things. I never know until it happens; I feel strongly that I am seeing what is going to occur. You and your children will be reunited this Friday."

Jillian flew out and landed in Hawaii Friday morning. The phone rang at 10:00 PM.

"Is Nancy there? This is Jillian's mother."

"Hi, it's me. How's Jillian?"

"She wants you to know the police arrested Joe and took the children to a youth holding center. She was brought there and stood facing an archway with a clock overhead. At exactly 4:00 PM, her three children walked under the arch and into her arms. We can't thank you enough." "I didn't do it; everyone did. I'm so happy for her, and for you."

As I was hanging up, the tears flowed and flowed. It was a total of 14 months since she had seen her children. I knew that there would be many adjustments and prices to pay for the damage to these innocent children. The next day, Lou called. He began filling me in. "They are all fine. Joe spent the night in jail while Jillian got on a plane with her kids. It's amazing; everything is just like you said. The children had clothes and shoes that were too tight. The middle one, her daughter, has three stitches on her upper lip from a dog bite. Joe's been living with a woman from the day he took them. She is now his wife. If you hadn't told us about the canceled checks, I would never have asked the lawyer to depose her and demand all her papers. Those papers at least confirmed that the bank he used was in Ramona,

California. Since there's no reciprocity yet between states, we waited months for the police out there to get the exact address and go to his home. Guess it was meant to be this way. I can't thank you enough. I'm going to get a great night's sleep tonight."

As I hung up, I mentally put my own family's situation in a beautiful light and prayed for a healthy outcome. My daughter's father was showing up in New York the following month for the custody suit. It had been a long, drawn-out preparation. I was as prepared as I could be; with over ten letters from psychotherapists and psychiatrists stating that I was emotionally healthy and a loving mother. Her teachers found me to be helpful and caring, whereas they found Gil to be threatening and scary and wouldn't allow him back to visit her in school. Her independent psychological testing showed a healthy young girl who was only afraid of one person, a man with dark hair and a dark mustache—her biological father. While brilliant and a very successful physician, his extreme response to his own emotional turmoil led him to consistently prove how brilliant he was. At the school, he demanded that these first graders answer his questions so he could determine if they were being taught well. He grilled Rebecca and would not hear the teachers asking him to be gentle. They wrote about it in letters for the court.

The following month, my daughter, Rebecca, and I went to court. If you saw the film, based on a true story, Kramer vs. Kramer, then you saw where we were. The courtroom scene was filmed in the courtroom that I sat in with my daughter, waiting to find out how just justice would be that day. I met Daniel Molinoff, the first lawyer to win a custody suit for a man (himself), in NY. Gil had hired him and, in 1979, had paid a small fortune to have the best in the country represent him. Gil had flown in from Montana and, as usual, strutted around with an aura of arrogance. Barry Birbrower, my lawyer, operating out of Peekskill, New York, was talking to Mr. Molinoff. When he saw me, he stopped and came over; we spoke for about five minutes.

The words didn't seem important, just everyday conversation. Strange stuff while waiting for outsiders, who will decide your life for you.

Molinoff joined us for a few minutes. He seemed pleasant and courteous; nothing stood out, and I wasn't tuning in, just trying to hold my ground. Molinoff excused himself and went to talk with Gil. Then he and Barry spoke alone. I saw Molinoff go over to Gil, and then, oddly, the two left the building. Barry was smiling as he spoke, "We're done here. Molinoff dropped the case after seeing your letters and meeting you. We were well prepared. I know a great restaurant, my treat."

Gil has since died of Dementia many years later. His obituary glows with his many great accomplishments as a physician/researcher and more. We all have our flaws. We can only pray that our flaws do not harm others.

Then, there are lawyers. Not always a great reputation, definitely a mixed bag. I've been blessed with having met some of the most generous and compassionate lawyers. Heart and soul are part of everything Barry did for us. He never sent a bill, yet he spent two years working to free us from our nightmare. Justice was really cooking that year.

Exercise: Touching Your Soul

The universe is large, and crime-solving is much more intense than predicting if someone is going to get married. Crimes trigger the heart of distrust and fear, reminding us how immature and problematical some of our species can be. That's one side. Creating a mental space to go to each time you are seeking to know about an intense, emotional situation is difficult. Start small, whatever that means to you. Pick a situation that is far removed from your life, yet, that you care about. Maybe a famine somewhere far away, or you pass an ambulance heading to a hospital; maybe an animal shelter makes a plea on television for adopting one of the homeless.

Begin by getting involved as a "healing agent." Open your hands (if you're not driving), your mind and heart and let the universal healing energies be sent through you to the situation. Concentrate your focus on sending, not receiving. Now the hard part...observe without emotions getting in the way, any thoughts, feelings, images, body sensations, and anything else that occurs. Do not interpret; just observe. The problem with most people isn't that nothing occurs; it's simply that the inner critic, the judgmental attitude, and the right/wrong thought process usually interrupts and takes over at that point. In order to survive, we pay attention to linear, rational thought; wait for the green light when crossing a street, stop at a red light while driving, etc. Unfortunately, our need to be approved of keeps the inner critic far too active and for most, at the wrong times. It is not meant to lead our lives, just to assist. Find a concept that allows you to take the negative thinking away from being front and center. What do you normally do if you want to escape in your mind from a situation? Pretend you are on a beautiful, peaceful island? Whatever you choose needs to be powerfully positive—enough to stop feeding the negative.

Record your impressions through words and drawings. Some things will not seem to have significance. It takes a lot of time and patience to get an overview of how your own mind functions. Removing unhealthy aspects of the need for approval takes time and patience. When enough of the self-disapproval is gone, our souls can feel and know life, consequently, we can apply the deeper inner wisdom that lies at the core of our being. Give it time. Give it room to grow. Water it daily with belief, even if part of you is arguing the point.

"Although the world is full of suffering,
it is also full of the overcoming of it." —Helen Keller.

Chapter 6

RACHEL

Gary Micco was on rotation as a detective in 1985 when I first made contact with him. A return visit in 1995 led to a greater understanding of how the police, or any investigator, can use the same intuitive powers that a psychic uses. If you have ever needed your own intuition to sort out a mystery—and who hasn't—then listen to Gary.

Gary spoke as if no time had passed, although it was a decade later. "I'll start with our initial contact through Ross English. I remember getting a piece of paper with your name and number on it; everything at the time was so hectic. I had no idea what it was about. We had this guy, a suspect, for about 14 hours, and we held him. We had a girl missing but didn't know what had happened. We had a dozen people say they saw his car. One lady said she saw him walking in the area where this girl lived. The girl had to walk home that day because she had missed the bus. So, we had this guy, and we had this girl missing, but we didn't know what happened.

"It started at 8:00 AM, in sleepy Long Valley. I came to work and started reading how the Yankees were doing in September when I was handed a note to give the vice-principal, a call on this missing girl. It appeared the day before in the blotter's reports. I called the vice-principal, and he said, 'What are you doing?'

'What are you talking about? I didn't get that far yet; it's only 8:05 AM.'

'She's missing, all of her friends are here, something's wrong.'

I said, 'I'll jump right on it.'

"Then, minutes later, I recalled a missing persons report on Rachel Domas; her parents called, and a patrolman followed it up and took the initial report the day before. We used to stop traffic and help her cross the street (the year before) when she was in eighth grade and for years before that when she was in the Long Valley Middle School. She passed me on the street coming up here. She used to walk back and forth to that school every day. We have a school post in the morning and afternoon to cross the kids safely.

"She's the sweetest girl you'll ever meet. I thought, runaway? She's so quiet, I didn't know all about her, but she wasn't the kind to run away. Then another note was handed to me by a dispatcher to call a woman from Fairview Avenue, which is where Rachel resided. I was supposed to call her. She had information. That was the first indication I had that a young man named Michael Manfredonia was seen in a green Volvo wagon, parked on Fairview Avenue less than a half a mile from Rachel's residence. She described this guy, who she thought worked at the local gas station, which at one point he did. Rachel would walk from her home and cut through the gas station towards school. So that was the first contact.

"I went to the man who owns the garage and gas station where Manfredonia worked. He said, 'I saw him that day. Matter of fact, we were driving cars on Fairview Avenue, testing some Volvos, and I saw his car.' Even the guy who worked there said he saw his car parked. Everyone we talked to saw his car. Usually, it's the other way around. Usually they say, 'We've seen nothing.'

"One person saw him walk, so after his name came up as an arrest in Chester Township, I called the sergeant there, and he said, 'yeah, we arrested him (Michael Manfredonia) for receiving stolen property, stolen from the garage where he worked.'

"This may have been why he was terminated. He wasn't an employee there when Rachel disappeared. Before hanging up, the sergeant said he would dig the file out on Michael. I told him I would stop by on my way to Michael's home. I hung up and called Michael Manfredonia's home, where I left a message to call me. A short while later, he (Michael) called me back, and I told him he was seen in the area of this missing girl's residence. He was seen there, his car was seen; we just wanted to know why he was there, trying to take the basic witness approach. Maybe he saw something; the guy was there in the neighborhood for hours. Michael was unresponsive, and we hung up. It had to be minutes later I got another call from the Chester Township sergeant; he said, 'He's here.'

"What?'

'He's here at headquarters, and he's saying he wants to know what the status of his community service is that he's been working off for a radar detector arrest.'

'Hang on to him, I want to talk to him.' So, I went down, introduced myself and said, 'would you help me out here? Come to my headquarters, and explain to me what you were doing the whole time.'

"He wrote this statement, two pages long, hand-written on how he was traveling down Fairview Avenue, left his house in Chester to go to the Quik-Chek in Flanders, off Bartley Road, to get cigarettes and soda. Drove back, took Bartley, then went to Naughright and down Fairview. His car broke down; he walked around for help. He went to the gas station for help. Then he left. I'm reading this, and I say, 'Hey, wait, how does your car break down? It was parked up a hill, off the road, a little wood road that went nowhere, about 200 feet long. How does your car break down, you back up a hill after it breaks down, you walk aimlessly for a couple of hours, you start up your car after that, and you drive home?

"I'll never forget reading that statement he signed. It made the hair stand up on the back of my neck. There was something so wrong. No one was thinking murder. No one. This is the morning, 11:00 AM; it began at 8:00 AM, so we had our guy a couple of hours later. I called George Deuchar; he and I were both in the detective bureau.

'Get here, now.'

'I'm right in the middle of Fire Prevention at a school,' George responded.

'Get here, now; we have a problem. Drop what you're doing.'

"He showed up. We held him (Michael), gave him a phone book, and said, 'If you want a lawyer, go look.' I opened it up to L and ceased questioning. We fed him, took care of him, held him, just detained him. We couldn't help but connect him to Rachel; his vehicle had been there, everyone said she missed the bus, a couple of neighbors said they saw her walking; one person saw her walking towards her house and saw Michael walking towards her. You've got him telling a bizarre story of how his car broke down. The prosecutor's office got involved. They looked for Rachel by checking the area by helicopter, cars, and on foot. Hours went by; we got nowhere. We drove him home; we had to let him go. It's a vast area, but we checked it: woods, fields, cornfields, rivers. She walked a couple of miles from the High School. So, at what point did she disappear? I felt, using common sense, that I knew where they would have met if they both walked at a normal pace. Michael never got a lawyer. We held him for 14 hours, and George Deuchar, and I brought him, completely exhausted, to his home. We held his car, took it and processed it. We didn't have a crime. I believe part of the case was lost because it had two phases. The first was a missing person's case, then a kidnapping. We let him go about 5:00 AM and George and I drove back to that area, the railroad bend, everything; you could just feel it in your bones. I think it was probably that day, that holding time, when I was handed a note to call Nancy."

Gary stopped talking, memories probably rolling in. I, too, sat remembering. Letting the puzzle reshape itself. Gary was filling in the missing pieces for me. I was looking back, telling him, "I can still see all the details of the events." They are ingrained in my mind. I knew one of the neighbors from a workshop I gave. That's why she called me. When she called, I had one of those awful sinking sensations that makes you wish you were still asleep. I asked for a photo of Rachel to stall and give me an hour to mentally and emotionally cope with taking some action. When she arrived, I offered her some tea, looked at the photo, and told her I needed to meditate on it. Unless you do the work yourself, you have no idea how it happens. For me, it's in an instant, for some people they quiet down and observe in a meditative state. I needed an excuse to be alone; I believed I knew Rachel's fate and who had caused it - now I wanted to see if the police needed whatever I had seen.

It was my turn to fill in some blanks for Gary, "I remember closing my bedroom door behind me and calling Detective Ross English. I told Ross I had a school yearbook brought in by a neighbor of the Domas family. I told him: 'I believe that a young man named Michael was Rachel Domas' murderer. He did it in one explosive moment of rage, strangled her, and dragged her into the woods first. Knew where she was, could see her lying there, could see somewhere else evidence of the struggle.

"Ross responded with, 'Let me call Long Valley, I haven't heard anything about this. Stay by the phone.' Five minutes later, Ross called; "She's missing all right. I've put a call in to Gary Micco; he's on the case. You should be hearing from him shortly. Can you get rid of the woman so you can talk easily?'

'I'll send her home.'

I continued, "Although I never look forward to lying, I don't consider it lying when I've picked up something, and it hasn't been proven yet. Entering the living room, I handed the yearbook back, saying, 'I'm never sure of how accurate my visions are, but in order to act on it, I need to reach out to those who can do the most good. I'm sorry, but telling you what I've seen in my mind serves no purpose. I can only promise you that I am doing whatever I can to help.'"

Gary continued the thread, "I remember calling you. I'll never forget hearing you tell me that you knew Rachel was dead, murdered, that someone was finding the body and would report in momentarily. We didn't even know. We had no body. Then you told me a young man named Michael did it. You went on to say he had a physical deformity, a wandering eye, and that he had worked at a gas station where he would see her going to and from school. Then you told me you could draw a picture of where Rachel was and where the evidence linking Michael to killing her could be found. I knew to meet with you, I would have to ask the prosecutor. I would have to wait until he came back. Before he could get back, Rachel's body was found just as you told me it would be. You had said she was strangled and dragged into the woods."

"Gary, as soon as you told me you didn't know if we could talk, I closed my emotional doors. I busied myself preparing dinner for my kids. You called back several hours later."

He continued, "Someone had discovered her body in the woods just where you said. Not knowing whether the murderer was on a killing spree, we were desperate to find him. You mentioned evidence. We needed to find it. The county prosecutor is saying, 'You know we can do this ourselves.' 'We should listen,' I repeated, and the chief of police put his arm around my shoulder and said, 'You do what you feel you have to do.' I called you within minutes. You said you wanted something that he touched or was with. I brought a noose because there was one point in the search of this dump area, we found this suicide note and noose. It was like a wire cable of some sort."

My turn to remember; "I knew I needed to be face to face with you, Gary. I also knew I couldn't speak the images; for some reason, I could only draw them."

"I felt I had to meet you." Gary was recalling. "Personally, I sensed it. I knew that anyone in law enforcement can't do any job by themselves. You know that when a citizen spots a license plate or a psychic has a vision. I don't care if it's the crazy woman who lives 200 miles away. You know the movie, *Missing Without a Trace*; no one listens to them. Listen to everyone. You have to."

Thinking of his comments, I responded, "Gary, I wish everyone felt that way. I remember as soon as you agreed to meet with me, more thoughts and images poured out. 'He, the kid who killed her, worked around the corner from her, but they hardly ever spoke. He's the kid no parents let their children be with. He's different, not part of any crowd, always alone. He left school last year and worked at a local garage pumping gas. Special educational needs, but mostly emotional. He saw her walking past the wooded lot going home from school and hated her. She represented everybody who ever made fun of him or snubbed him. He grabbed her, and she resisted. He's much stronger than her; he took her by the throat and dragged her into the mountainous woods, where he promptly killed her. That's where you found her body; I can show you where. Father drives a pickup truck. That's all I got.' That was our first conversation after you called and told me they discovered her body."

"Right," Gary's vision seemed far away when he spoke, "they had just found her body...in the woods...no evidence around and...though we picked Michael up for questioning that morning, without a body, we had to let him go. Then with the body found, we couldn't find him."

Two families were devastated. Lots of dear friends would mourn a sweet young girl's horrible meeting with death. No one can make sense of such pain. Anyone who talks about everyone choosing their path has never been a crime victim. No one chooses that path, no one except the perpetrator, who couldn't possibly be listening to their own soul. Perhaps the choices are not about whether we become someone's victim, but if we do, what we let it do to us, whether here on earth or beyond.

I remember when I was six years old when we moved to a new neighborhood in the East Flatbush section of Brooklyn. Moving day came, and at six years of age, I wasn't of much help. A boy and girl rang our bell and asked to play with me. I suppose my parents felt grateful to them and let me go outside. I didn't want to. I hated meeting new people. Now, I was sitting on the first porch I ever sat on, and with strangers. I could hardly hear them, and I didn't want to talk. I remember them telling me they lived across the street, next door to each other. I was so shy I didn't say a word. They kept talking, and I kept hoping it would be over so I could see my new room being set up. I watched them as they turned to see another boy walk past us on the street. The boy sitting next to me called out, "There goes four eyes," and the girl laughed. My shyness was thrown out by my fury. I knew what it meant.

"If you are going to talk like that, you can't stay here with me," I yelled at them. "Everyone has a handicap, only some you can see and some you can't. Don't make fun of anyone in front of me. I don't like it." My voice was the loudest I had ever heard it. I sat, surprised at my voice. The thoughts that darted out of my mouth were as clear to me as the cloudless sky. The two children muttered an apology to me.

"I'm not the one you hurt." I was furious. It was the first time I ever remembered being angry. They called out, "Sorry," loud enough for the other boy to hear and then quickly left. I had not made any friends that day. I was very proud of my anger. It was nice to care. Maybe I wasn't the selfish child my mother told me I was. I jumped off the porch and skipped into the house. I didn't care if anyone liked me; I liked myself.

It was a discovery that planted a seed that took decades to grow.

In the fourth grade, I suddenly began walking with a limp. My hip hurt almost all the time. My parents took me to our family physician, who could not find anything. His conclusion was that I was faking it to get attention. He had admitted my sister to a hospital earlier that year. She had polio in the legs. The only explanation he could come to was that I was mimicking her. He told my parents I probably needed some attention. Although the limp faded over the next few months, and my parents assumed he was right; years later, in reviewing a spinal tomogram, I could see the congenital deformities that led to my limp.

It was only my devotion from age three to the field of classical ballet that kept my muscles sufficiently strong and stretched enough to balance and compensate for the spine and missing disc. The story told about my childhood by the adults was that the only thing I ever really asked for was dancing lessons. I started asking at age two, and, by three they gave in. Perhaps my inner teacher was working through me even then. These lessons that I took until age 13 taught me to instinctually understand movement. This has served to help me learn to restore function again and again, despite extensive injuries incurred at the hands of others. I believe my love and devotion to dance has literally kept me out of a wheelchair. With all the possibilities that present themselves, I've never lost the ability to care for myself and others. I believe that may be why I can feel Michael and his issues and can feel Rachel and her pain.

Gary continued to remember, "I asked you to meet me at 10:00 PM. We would meet halfway. I picked the church off Naughright. Do you recall?"

"Very well," I answered. "I was incredibly nervous. I had agreed to meet a stranger late at night in a dark place. By the time I arrived at the parking lot, my imagination had destroyed my nervous system. I was terrified. Your white car with the red bubbles on top helped calm me. I pulled up alongside, and with handbag in hand, got in the front seat of your car. The interior was lit. I liked your eyes immediately; they were filled with concern and compassion."

Gary remembers, "After you pulled up in your car, and came into mine, talked and broke the ice, I gave you the wire. You immediately said, 'He's heavily drugged with some over-the-counter pharmaceutical.' Nancy, I was trying to find him; that was my purpose for meeting with you. We're trying to find him. Where the hell is he? You kept looking away, like you were seeing something far away as you spoke, 'There's grass around him, you can't see him, but he can see you. He's on a hill; there is a body of water around or near him, whether it be a puddle or a lake I can't tell. There's also a fifty-gallon drum.' Then you drew a diagram of where the drum was. You drew where a piece of her jewelry and torn clothing could be found. I now understood why you had to draw. The evidence was in hundreds of acres of hilly woods. You even included several garbage cylinders and an idea of what particular garbage was lying on the ground. I couldn't miss it. Then I asked you, 'Where is Michael?' You immediately responded with, 'Whoops, he's ill. He took an overdose of some over-the-counter sedative to kill himself. He wants to go home. He's on a hilltop looking down at his home. He's waiting to see his father's truck. He'll come down when his father comes home. He needs him. Wait a minute; his house is being watched. It's a bunch of cop cars. You know his house is being watched, don't you? He's going to be caught very soon; he's beginning to come down the hill. You've got the house surrounded, waiting for him!' Just then, the sergeant came on the radio announcing that he (Michael) was coming down the hill and entering the house. I gunned the car and you jumped out and ran to your car.

"The next day, I took the map with me and figuratively stood on it, by the fifty-gallon drum. I looked around, and there was everything you laid out on the map, exactly as I was seeing it around me. I rushed to the scene. He (Michael) was picked up at the house, and rushed to the squad room in Long Valley, where I jumped in the ambulance and read him his Miranda rights. He was, without a doubt, out of it. At the hospital, they pumped his stomach because he had taken something like Tylenol Cold tablets, a zillion of them. I don't remember. After his stomach was pumped, we read him his rights again at the hospital. The first thing in the hospital, it was dark, and he looked at me; he was lying in bed, he had a tube down to his stomach still pumping stuff, and he was the 'fraidest thing I ever saw. I said, 'It's time to talk about it.' He had told me in the ambulance, 'It's time to talk about it.' He was sitting up in the hospital bed with a look on his face, and he said, 'I was driving down the road and my car broke down, and I parked it, and I got out to take a leak, I looked down and there she was.' He covered his eyes as he said that; as he put his hands on his face, he screamed, 'There she is, there she is, she's a bloody mess.' I interjected quickly, 'What did you do?' He continued, 'I, I, I, grabbed her, I dragged her, I buried her, sticks, rocks,' his voice was frantic, 'whatever I could find, I ran, I ran.' That was basically as far as we got. Not, 'I did it to her,' but 'I found her, there she is, bloody mess, I'm scared, I don't know what to do. The following day, Monday is when he confessed. He was found guilty and given a life sentence.

"Nancy, I never told the prosecutor about you. That would have been my job. I hope you understand. Everything was as if you were there. When I put the evidence on the prosecutor's desk, he said, 'See, you didn't need her.'"

"Gary, it was over; at least that part. The families' grief was just starting; for Michael's and Rachel's families, friends, and relatives. I remember praying myself to sleep that night. Lucid dreams have been my way for the longest time. While the dream takes place, my conscious self is able to notice that I am dreaming. Sometimes I will be busy interpreting the messages while the dream occurs. That night, I just prayed to help one very gentle, sweet soul who did not have a chance to say goodbye to her loved ones. Her dreams were shattered far more than mine or yours. Now she needs peace."

Exercise: *Soaking Up the Scene*

Opening your mind to encounters with the dark side has long been a subject of study. Humans have always been both fascinated and horrified by the consequences of rage. I believe it is partly a desire to protect ourselves from harm and to see it coming. We seek mysteries, from the core of the earth to the farthest reaches of the galaxies, to solve the mystery of life. Perhaps life is constantly being created, and the more we peel back the layers, the more we get a glimpse of the unknown. It would be wonderful not to know the dark side of human behavior, that is, if it didn't exist. Unfortunately, it does, and so do we. Each of us who don't want to participate or be "tainted" by the horrors can put our hearts and minds to the task of surrounding every horrible situation. Focus universal love, fully embracing the feelings without fear, we could create miracles. Getting close to someone's rage is like sticking our hands in a flame; recovery is completely dependent on our core beliefs!

Here's an example from both Gary Micco's work with me and

his own that followed. Gary Micco tells a story that is wondrous proof that we are truly all connected. When we believe we are harmless and seek only to serve all of life, I believe we are inherently giving ourselves permission to dial the universal number for all living things. Oddly enough, we can dial it through holding inanimate or animate things, such as keys, a necklace, an envelope containing a letter—even one that is a copy or perhaps a fingerprint. This story is about a fingerprint.

Gary recalls, "There was a burglary of a pharmacy in Long Valley. October 17, 1986. Long Valley Pharmacy; it's a plaza, it had double doors, and then fifteen feet of window, running parallel to these doors, as high as these doors. The bottom part of the left window is broken and smashed. The subject goes in, and steals $800 in cash, a couple of thousand pain killers, Dilaudid, Demerol, Percodan, and so forth. Walk around the scene, survey the scene, back at the port of entry, pull out the fingerprinting kit, and dust for prints; we find an index finger, tip of an index finger, half of the last joint on a piece of broken glass. We lift it and keep the lift. We look through every known suspect; we're striking out."

"I go to Nancy and, remembering the homicide case I figured she needed something of the guy. I got the guy's fingerprints; this is cool. So, I walk in with this file without telling Nancy about it except for a basic one liner, something like, 'Someone broke into a store.' I handed her the print and she said she had never held a fingerprint before. She started flipping it around saying this is wild, she's sitting Indian style with her cats, and flipping through this thing. She described a person, she said he was in his twenties, probably late twenties, strange-looking, pock marked skin, and he had a deformity with the left side of his body. His left arm had a problem. She said we would get him; he's a drug addict, he will do it again and again. She concluded by saying he became addicted because of the pain in his arm and muttered about doctors who don't really care or teach pain management."

"Almost one year later to the day I read a bulletin, Morris County Prosecutor's Office; a guy was arrested in New Jersey for pharmacy burglaries. I ran the print for a match, and got a hit. I remember exactly what Nancy described to me about this person and could now verify. His father brought him in to be served with the warrants here at headquarters. He showed up, walked through the door, and there he was, pock-marked skin, 29 years old, and deformed on the left side of his body. In taking the mug shots of him, I could see his arm was wiped out. I learned it was from a propeller accident. He had taken painkillers and became addicted. He wasn't a criminal before the accident. I don't know if he came out of the hospital a drug addict. Maybe he did drugs then and left the hospital okay. Maybe he was walking around feeling crappy one day and decided that the drug did make him feel good; let's go back and do that."

"I'm not a hard-nosed street cop with a big male ego who has to do it all himself. I am a resourceful person who will use whatever is given to me; in terms of getting the goal accomplished. Gratefully, I'll add. There are people who help me achieve whatever I have to achieve. From a law enforcement standpoint, Nancy is a hell of a tool. I would absolutely recommend using her on a case. I'm not talking about any psychic; forget about the vision part of it. I believe anyone can develop that ability. She's a bright person. She can plug herself into a situation and feel it, be there. When a detective goes to a crime scene, he needs to do that at the crime scene before he pulls his camera out and throws the dust around; forget it. When a detective goes to a crime scene, and he's looking for the bad guy, he better put all his equipment down, open his eyes, open his ears, and walk around the scene. We're trained to look around for evidence, not for the feel of the place. Nancy's way of seeing has rubbed off on me. Taking the tool that you have, the ability you have. I got a call about a burglary where people were away for a week and got back. A weapon was taken, a lot of jewelry, and some money. I showed up at the house at about 3:00 PM. The port of entry was a broken window in the back of the house, entry through the kitchen. Just before they left for vacation, they cleaned and vacuumed the rugs; cleaned everything. You don't pick up the camera, you don't pick up the dusting equipment; you sit everyone down. Of course, you've got to preserve the scene, the evidential aspect of it."

"You walk around the house, see what you feel, see what you see, don't just look at it, soak in it, feel it, be the guy. Recall Caddy Shack, be the ball man, I remember that. Be the ball, you're walking through the house, and I said to myself, 'Yes, you've got one guy here,' because here we have the port of entry, the kitchen, and we can cut through the dining room to get to the stairs. "

"This guy makes a beeline through the dining area with work boot tracks. Cool, we can follow him. You walk upstairs to the right; the master bedroom is to the left at the end of the house. Look at his stride; he even skipped a couple of stairs; he knew where he was going. Make a right; he went into a girl's room. Beds all messed up, drawers pulled out, footprints, footprints, footprints. Forget about fingerprints; who needs them? Look at this, he then makes one trip down the hall, stops at a boy's room, picks up some sort of toy, a ball perhaps, then goes to the master bedroom, takes some jewelry, takes a gun. So, we see where the stuff is being taken. I can just walk in his footsteps, because of spending time with Nancy. Not only what she sees and feels, but her ability to teach someone. Not that I was there to be taught, but as I said, unless you listen, you won't hear it; or watch and pick it up."

"Well, we went to the father. We see a great deal of interest in the girl's room. The father said his daughter is 19. Tell me about your daughter. She's a student, attractive, and he hands me her picture. She's got several boyfriends. I say, 'Name them.'"

"This poor man starts pulling names out of a hat. He rolled them out fast, 'Billy, Bobby, Tommy, Johnny, Smith, Eddy,' 'Smith, stop,' I said. Smith, why Smith? Something just stood out. 'Tell me about Smith. Yeah, tell me about him, what's he drive, etc.' Then basic police work kicked in. Go to the neighbor's house. 'Seen any vehicle there?'

'Oh yeah, for two days, I saw this vehicle.' She describes it. Go back to the father. 'What does Smith drive?' He describes the same vehicle the neighbor just described. Smith was there for two days, staying at the house. Smith knew they were on vacation. I have the girl call her friend who knows Smith. The friend says, 'Yeah, he was target practicing at a quarry in the woods recently, with a 22.' It's missing from this house. Picked him up in two hours."

"We need all the equipment; we need the stuff we're shown in the police academy, I'm impatient, so sometimes my downfall is I don't know when to stop, I should know when, but I don't; I want to get to the end. If you hand me a letter and it has a summary, I'll go to the summary."

"Observation and soaking up the scene. It can be taught to others. If I had never met Nancy, it's probably something I might have developed at some point. It also gives you more self-confidence; boosts you a bit. Not to pretend I'm psychic because I don't think I am or pretend to be when I'm walking around the house, but to walk through and observe and soak it in at work, before you even begin to pick up the equipment you were taught to use, you better know how to use that part of you."

Now understand the following account that occurred for me, then write your own story of either a true-life encounter with love being victorious or one from your imagination.

I was in a health food store, pouring over books, when a young man, dressed in white, quietly spoke, "Don't touch that book, it's from the devil."

"Thank you, but I am not afraid of the devil." My voice was clear, direct, and strong.

"Please don't speak so loudly; he can hear you."

"Who, the devil?" again at normal range.

Even quieter, "Yes, shhh."

"Okay, if you can answer these questions, I'll consider your concerns. Do you believe in Christ?"

"Absolutely."

"And, of course, God?"

"Absolutely."

"Isn't God the Creator of All?"

"Absolutely."

"Don't you believe that God is the most powerful force there is?"

"Absolutely."

"Then how can you be afraid of any of God's creations? I don't get it. Isn't love more powerful than fear?"

"Where did you learn that? Can we go talk?"

That was an encounter with someone who believed himself to be extremely spiritual and religious; for me, he was simply a powder keg holding onto some belief ferociously, terrified of letting go. If he ever had to suddenly let go, I wouldn't want to see the violence that might follow, either towards himself or others. Helping him come to his own beliefs, where real faith and love can withstand the destructive forces; that is mine and everyone's responsibility. Now, it's your turn. Write about an encounter with the dark side that leaves you feeling hope for humankind.

"Hope is being able to see that there is light despite all of the darkness." —Desmond Tutu.

Chapter 7

A VISION OF MURDER

"Enid, I feel awful; I see a husband killing his wife." Enid and I were mutual friends of Shirley and Harvey. I was driving us to their home as we talked.

"My God, not Shirley and Harvey?" Enid's face turned a shade paler than I had ever seen.

"No, not them; it's weird; it feels like it is connected to them somehow. I can't tell who, though."

We had pulled up to their house. I attempted to recover my balance, and we went in to spend a peaceful lunch in a beautiful, mountainous area of New Jersey where we could see miles of greenery. That night, lying in bed, I couldn't stop thinking of the thought of a husband killing a wife. The next day, I called Shirley and told her what was obsessing my every moment. She had no information to add except that she was glad it wasn't about them.

That was in the middle of August 1986. Seven days later, I was driving alone to Shirley and Harvey's. *All gone*, I thought. No more murder feelings. Getting out of my car, no need to lock it here; I walked up to the glass door. Harvey was standing there with a strange unreadable face.

"Ellen was murdered this morning. Brad and Robin are devastated. Would you go talk with them?" Harvey sounded as devastated as he looked.

Reeling from the impact, I now knew all the pieces. Back in July, I went with Harvey and Shirley to their neighbor's house to meet a new employee, hired directly from China.

"Her name is Ellen; she's 40 years old, sweet, and special. We were told that she has wanted to come to America since she was a little girl. Would you like to meet her?" Ellen was outside talking with Brad and Robin when we were introduced. I walked over to her, smiling, and she ran into my arms. I held her to me, and when we broke apart, we walked arm in arm into the house. We did not speak the same verbal language, but obviously, we communicated deeply with each other. I left her my number on a slip of paper and told her if she ever wanted company, please call. We were friends. Walking out, I remember Shirley's strange look and comment, "I've never seen someone of Chinese descent so effusive with someone they just met." That was the only time Ellen and I would be together.

Brad called and asked me to come to their home a week later. In my mind, it had been a murder of a wife. Was Ellen married? Sitting with Brad and Robin, Brad filled in the details. Ellen was married; it was an arranged marriage to a Chinese man who lived in Brooklyn. She had agreed to annul the as-of-yet, unconsummated marriage once she was living in the US. She had also agreed to pay him a sum of $500 a month for several months. When Charlie, a friend of Brad's, drove her in, Mr. Wang, her husband, asked Charlie to please wait downstairs. I don't know why he agreed to it; Ellen was afraid of Mr. Wang. Charlie went downstairs. With much forethought, Mr. Wang took a knife and butchered a lovely gentle woman. He then called the police and told them they had an argument that led to a violent quarrel. As I listened, all I could do was console Brad and Robin. I reminded them that whatever time Ellen had in America, her dream had come true.

We agreed that I would come back in a few days and look at the situation. This was being done in friendship. There was an understanding that there was to be no monetary consideration for any work I would do for them. Three days later, my daughter accompanied me to their home. The neighbors, Brad and Robin, took us to the back deck. Sitting amongst beautiful mountains and lush gardens, the subject matter I felt and saw in my mind's eye changed the feel of everything for me. Words poured out as I saw visions again, "Mr. Wang had hurt her before, didn't he? In fact, I feel he had been here."

"Yes, we found him lurking around and then found out that he went into Ellen's quarters and made her sleep in a chair while he slept in the bed," Brad was very matter of fact. "He then tried to strangle her. She came crying to us, and we threw him off the property."

"Good, then there is a police report. That would make my work go easier," I breathed a sigh of relief.

"No, we didn't call the police. He left." Again Brad was unemotional.

"But he tried to kill her then. Okay, listen, it's still important that the Brooklyn D.A.'s office is told this information."

"Why should I tell them that?"

"Because it's proof that it was premeditated and that it was not a case of a domestic dispute. He will try to prove it as domestic; you have to fight him on it. Otherwise, bail could be affordable, and he'd be out." My mind was still dealing with their knowledge of a previous attempt and their lack of filing a report.

"Do you think that he would come back here? Don't say he would." Robin's scared voice cut in.

"Robin, do you want me to tell you what I believe and feel, or do you want me to stop? I know it's frightening, but it's more frightening when you don't deal with what you have. Then you have no control at all. Mr. Wang would love to steal from you; he saw your place. Your best protection is a high bail. He'll never get out or even get to trial. I see him dying of a heart attack in jail. If you don't help, he could get out, and then I would suggest you have your place under round-the-clock guard."

"Stop talking like that. Why do you want me frightened?" Robin, pregnant and normally easily frightened, became more protective. Shock will send folks into extreme responses.

"Robin, I didn't kill Ellen; I'm trying to help resolve it. Do whatever you want, but I wouldn't pretend this man would only harm Ellen and no one else."

With that, Rebecca and I left. "Why are they nasty to you?" Rebecca's voice reminded me of how often, as a messenger, I became the scapegoat early in my life. As a nurse and as a patient, I got to see how some folks would be so thoughtful of others even while they were frightened, sometimes in excruciating pain, while others would take out their fears on us by demanding, yelling, and sometimes attempting to be extremely inappropriate. People show who they are in crisis—thoughtless or thoughtful.

If only they had called the police the first time. Even if nothing else would had been accomplished, they would have clearly come to terms with not letting her go upstairs alone to that man's apartment. How could they? My voice got loud and furious. Ellen died because no one had the courage to take action against someone willing to attempt to take a life.

A week later, Brad sent me a copy of his letter to the DA's office. He believed me. The DA told him that Mr. Wang had told his barber days before, that he was going to kill his wife. Bail was set high, and Mr. Wang could not post it. Several weeks later, Brad called to tell me that Mr. Wang had died in jail of a heart attack.

Ellen's situation and death brought childhood pains to the surface. I always felt like a stranger where everyone else knew life. Maybe Ellen felt our similarities more than our differences. It took decades to shed most of the shyness that had captured me early on. Ellen did not have the opportunity to live long enough to shed hers. I hope she hears my love for her strong and deep. She is a soul sister who left too soon.

Exercise: Dismiss Nothing

This is the toughest challenge. Believing in your own experience, even when you are not liked for it. There is an odd twist here. Delusions are not to be found only among the truly psychotic. We can all convince ourselves of anything when we put our minds to it. We can lie to ourselves, and with shame as our strongest internal response, we can invent a fantasy of what is happening and discard reality. How to tell when you are fooling yourself? I don't know. Because of possible hidden agendas, we can read into our feelings, information that isn't accurate. I know a man who fell in love with a woman who clearly told him she would only be his friend. For twenty years, and lots of therapists, meditation, etc.… he kept up the mental charade of picking apart every word and deed coming from her. He would convince himself she really loved him; why couldn't she just admit it? Was he delusional or simply refused to hear the truth? She remained friends with him, always and only platonic. He was invited to her wedding; when he became ill, she would visit and offer help. She definitely cared about him, just not the way he cared for her. How many partnerships, love, and business relationships break apart because one partner speaks directly and the other hears only what they want to hear? Learning to listen and be completely present in each moment helps strip away layers of defensive delusions, ridiculous assumptions, and, best of all, layers of anxiety.

With any work that involves handling the darkest side of human nature, a belief system that helps you regain trust in a divine, universal, loving connection will help you recover peace in your heart and mind. I can suggest that trusting your intuition, your gut feeling, and the flashes of words and images that are bestowed internally takes a willingness to confront who you are, the good, the bad, the beautiful, and the ugly. Ready?

Thoughts, feelings, images, and any sensations that are out of context to the situation need to be noticed. For instance, you walk into a restaurant where you are meeting a friend, nothing unusual; you've done this dozens of times. This time, you are overcome with anger and feel edgy as you sit down to wait. If this is not the way you usually handle a five-minute wait—stop—ask yourself to slow down and breathe deeply. Be willing to discover what fears are trying to surface. No answer? That's okay, get out your journal, piece of scrap paper, or smartphone and record the date, time, place, circumstance, and your response. Notice I didn't say reaction. You are unconsciously participating in an event that your conscious mind isn't immediately capable of recognizing or facing.

When my son was still in a car seat and my daughter was in kindergarten, I was driving from my home in Peekskill, NY, to downtown Peekskill. Jesse, my son, was in the back seat, happily pretending he was driving. I was singing along with the voice on the radio. As I came to a full stop at the bottom of the hill, I looked to the left, then to the right. I was going to turn left. On the right-hand corner was a car dealership. About 75 feet away, at the far end of the car dealership, a man in a business suit was talking with a local police officer. I saw them and panicked. Instead of turning left towards town, I quickly turned right and gunned my gas pedal, flying down the road. Within a few seconds, I heard a sound I still hear—gunshots.

Returning home, I was overcome with guilt and shame. Running away is not a style I respect in myself, unless it's a fire (yes, I've been in one).

The radio announced that two gunmen robbed the bank on Main Street. That was the bank I would have passed had I turned left. Upon leaving the bank and seeing the police officer, they shot him. He was shot in the abdomen and lying in the local hospital. The gunmen were caught the same day. A few days later, I drove down the same roads to do my own investigation. Had I turned left, I would have probably been in the line of sight of the gunmen. Had I not sped upon turning right, the line of fire would have been by my son's head. I still freak out at the thought. It was an incredible lesson.

Sometimes, the body/mind does not have the time to inform the conscious mind of what's going on. Sometimes, the conscious mind cannot handle or interpret what is happening. We call it freaking out. The less fear, the clearer the message.

Keep wrapping yourself in the Light that connects all life in a loving manner. Step into the world of light waves and imagine for a moment that you can see the energy of the universe passing through all matter, stones, tables, humans, ants...everything. The rhythm of the light wave is interrupted by other energies that disrupt the power of the life force. Auras are descriptions of the flow of light and the changes in its rhythm due to physiological, emotional, mental, spiritual, and environmental information. Catalytic toxins, whether they are poisonous substances or poisonous thoughts, break up the flow and create muddy colors.

Using techniques of your own, or those described in the chapter on healing, start tuning into the colors of people and animals throughout your day. When you are suddenly in the grip of a strong emotion that seems to come from nowhere, check your environment for its aura. If you start seeing brownish red coming from somebody (human or animal), remove yourself if possible. Unlike the bright reds that speak of personal love and vitality, muddy red streaks in an aura indicate rage. Unbeknownst to my conscious mind, my spirit had seen the aura of the situation in Peekskill and guided my son and I to safety.

I'm lightly entering the topic of energy fields, auras, etc. A quick overview is that the light wave passes through everything; with many layers of moving energy, we have different frequencies throughout the fields of life. More on that in an upcoming book, *The Inner Journey's Guidebook*.

We can't possibly figure out all the right moves, the right places to be, or the right thing to say. We can develop a healthy trust of our soul's guidance, and a respect and devotion to the source of life that guides us through our own individual WuLi (patterns of organic energy). For a great read, try Gary Zukavs' first book, *The Dancing WuLi Masters*. It is a layman's interpretation of physics. Somehow it struck a chord in me and assisted me in believing that every encounter offers an opportunity to become a master of the dance of life. An easier read is Gary's book *Seat of the Soul*.

"I shine my light on every dark thought that arises, and they turn into whispers with wings and fly away." —Jodi Livon.

Chapter 8

MURDER CLOSE TO HOME

A local detective called to ask me if I would take a look at the recent murder of a 42-year-old divorcee. The police had some interesting leads and were curious to see if my psychic vision would match their hunches. This case was close to home, about a mile from where I had lived. It was a woman I had seen in the local bar where I danced to live music on Thursday nights with a group of friends. I always loved dancing, ballet, toe, modern, rock, and live music always created the most fun for me.

I did not know the woman but remembered her face. Pretty lady. Not so pretty were the photos of her brutal murder. As usual, the police would not tell me anything. I asked if I could go to the murder scene. It was strange going there. I had lots of friends in that apartment complex. Walking past the crime scene tape reminded me how unsafe the world can be.

As I walked from the car, I had a nasty feeling that I could feel as a physical sense. I knew it was not coming from inside me, but rather from something off toward my right. I turned towards that direction and saw a gazebo. As I stared, a grayish cloud-filled shape that I felt as a male presence, was there. It was the energy that told me it was someone who could kill. I could tell by the jaggedness and discoloration of the field. I had my first clue. I tuned into the energy and started directing questions to it, knowing that it was a way to link to the mind of the killer.

The first question I asked was, "Did you know the victim?" "No," he shot back. The "he" was not yet visible; the sound was male. I could feel him watching her from the gazebo, so I deduced that he probably stalked her the night he killed her. They will not shield from the link we send as long as it does not pose a threat. I kept my heart open as I worked, knowing love is the strongest and best tool I could ever use. This all took place in the space of time needed to walk about 50 feet to the door of the apartment. Other police from the state were there. They were ready to listen, though not necessarily believe, but I was used to that. I walked around the apartment, and although I didn't show emotion, a wave of horror and sadness swept over me as I saw the aftereffects of the crime.

The woman's body had been removed, but the blood remained all over the living room wall from floor to ceiling. It was while staring at the wall that I saw a scene unfold. Her teenaged daughter heard something in her sleep and went out into the living room, only to discover her mother lying against the living room wall with blood everywhere. She ran out of the apartment screaming. Walking into her daughter's room, my eyes went to the ceiling. It was covered with angry writing in red, expressing hatred and fury at her mother and the world. I smiled and remembered when I let my daughter crayon her bedroom wall in our apartment. My daughter was an artist early on, and she did palm trees, suns—happy images. Yet I knew if she was upset and wrote on walls, I would know it was simply to release those feelings. It was obvious to me that her mother loved her and gave her daughter room to express even what was uncomfortable for both of them. I walked back into the living room, ready to share what I felt and saw.

"It was a young man who uses drugs, roams at night, was high when he killed her, and never met her. He lives in the next town, Netcong. He came in through the kitchen window, fast. Too fast for her to do anything. He immediately attacked her. He was looking for someone to cut up. He's done quite a few petty crimes, mostly stealing."

The police obviously felt differently. They were talking now. They were torn between it being the daughter, whom they felt hated her mother and thought her mother was a tramp (their word, not mine), or perhaps "one of the mother's string of lovers." Not so, I told them. She did not sleep around. She was searching for a permanent relationship and did not always choose wisely. She was honest enough to admit it and break it off when she realized it was not right for her. I continued, "She tried to maintain friendships with the men after she left them, and some of them were still her friends. It did not mean she slept with them any longer. Her daughter was going through difficulties over not having a family life and normal mother-daughter issues." The state police and I obviously clashed on our opinions. They reiterated that she played around and probably let in "One of her many lovers. She was a tramp." My only comment was simple, "If any of you played around, what would we call it?"

I had not heard that word since adolescence. They would not be easy to convince. I let it go and told the detective I knew to please take me home. It would be pointless to fight their beliefs about women. Not being believed came naturally to me. Years of therapy and meditation had erased most of the pain, but nothing would ever remove the memories. In today's world, I take to writing blogs, books, and more. It helps convert wounded feelings from my childhood and young adult years into valuable hindsight.

My mind stopped back flashing as the detective, and I got into his olive green Chevy. Disbelief of anyone I feel is innocent immediately begins a movie of my past. The detective looked at me, saying, "You don't think it was the daughter?"

"Not at all," was my reply. "Look, if you are planning to interview the girl, please go gently. She is devastated and terrified."

"We plan to give her a polygraph."

"Please don't. Get her help first. You will destroy her ability to heal if you press her on this. She will retreat into a silent world where she won't be reached for a long time."

"I can't go on that."

This detective and I had been friends for a while, and although he would go ahead with the plans, he was willing to share that piece of information. Not only was the daughter devastated by the mother's murder, with plenty of her own guilty feelings (I believed they had just argued that day), but she was a definite suspect in their eyes! Not knowing who killed her mother, she had to be pretty terrified for her own life. That was the first and last meeting with the police on the case for me.

Through friends who were working as local reporters, I heard that the daughter was given a lie detector test and passed. No other word came until approximately three months later, when a 19-year-old Netcong resident was picked up for petty theft and later confessed to the murder of this girl's mother. He was booked and found guilty of first-degree murder. The report told of his drug history. Months later, at a lecture I was giving, I spoke about the lack of intuition and compassion on the part of those particular officers. Of course, the flip side is that they needed to rule her out or in. That's their job. I kept wishing they went with healthier hunches. A woman came up to me when the lecture was finished. She was a close friend of the dead woman's family and thanked me. The daughter was so traumatized by not only the murder, but by authorities who believed she was possibly guilty, that she left the state to live with relatives. I was also told that she became a recluse, unable to communicate with the outside world.

Many years later, I received a call from this girl who was now an adult and married. She came to my home, where we spoke about her mom and the tough time this precious girl had. She wanted me to know that she knew that I believed her and that it helped. I was grateful to this woman who had lost so much. Yet she wanted whatever positive connection she could have with the past. That is the mark of an exceptional woman who has made it through some of the most difficult and painful experiences imaginable.

Exercise: Slipping into New Perceptions

Through the veil we go, slipping past the illusions and the mask of seeking approval. The feel of a situation does not necessarily make any sense to the conscious mind. If we seek too much approval from the outside world, a conflict between our sense of things and what is expected of us develops. To be successful in crime-solving is to care to help more than anything else. That does not automatically mean you can call the police (if you are not one yourself), and they should listen to you. It also does not mean that you will be liked or applauded for helping. Can you live with that? Can you live with not talking about whatever work you are doing, except with those involved? If you believe you are ready to help, the next step is to wait. Unless you have a great relationship with somebody in law enforcement or are in it yourself, you can easily be turned away. There are not many citizens who work with the police, FBI, etc. Why?

From my own personal experience, and the experiences of others I've encountered, there is a simple answer. How does someone in law enforcement know you are the real thing when they themselves usually don't know anything about the psychic world? Most people get in through their previously established credentials; someone who they respect has told a person involved in a criminal investigation that there is a person who is very psychic and could possibly help. If that doesn't happen for you and you believe in the work, consider entering one of the fields of law enforcement like Gary Micco; use your intuitive faculties as a professional.

During my student nursing days at Brooklyn College, I heard a concept that has endeared itself into my life, particularly when I believe I am there to help. Mrs. Norman, my first teacher in nursing, put it eloquently and yet simply, "Before entering the room of a person in need, put all your own problems in a bag by the door and leave them there until you walk out. If you still need to carry them, pick them up after you are completed with your work." That is one of the clearest premises I have ever heard. Get the ego's need out of the way, relying totally on your humanitarian attitude, and go!

Years later, I still internally create a conscious statement of what I am about before I enter into anyone else's spiritual domain. It goes something like this: "May my presence and all my senses express only the divine through each and every moment, movement, expression, and feeling."

Create your own internal spiritual concept, one that connects you, lovingly, to all of life—even those you fear. Create a system of belief that allows you to walk in the light no matter how difficult the situation. Love is the greatest power. Write your own powerful belief that permits you to know your soul and, through that, everyone else's.

"Love is the beauty of the soul." —Saint Augustine.

Chapter 9

SERIAL KILLER

"Hi, Nancy, this is Louise. You may not remember me. We met at Margaret's house this summer," the voice on the phone said. I'm always grateful when someone gives me a clue so I can put a face to the voice.

"My daughter Katy's friend, Amy Hoffman, is missing. Amy worked last night at the Morris County Mall, and her car was found there with the door open."

Louise entered my life in the summer of 1982 when my friend Margaret, whom I have known since the eighth grade, invited me to her daughter's Bat Mitzvah. Leaving the temple, we followed them back to their house, where I promptly piled food on a paper plate. With a drink in one hand and chipmunk cheeks, I grinned my hello to a couple who introduced themselves as Dr. George and Louise Williams. George has a Ph.D. in psychology, and Louise was attending Rutgers University in New Jersey. She was studying a rare tumor as part of her thesis in microbiology. Louise was excited to talk to a psychic, and George was squinting his disbelief. She had heard me on a radio show with Candy Jones about a month earlier. It was a friendly chat, and then we all moved on to speak to others.

Months went by, and the summer heat had changed to a brisk cold chill. I was preparing Thanksgiving dinner for my children and myself when the phone rang. It was Louise. As she spoke, an image drifted dead center where I could not hide from it. A naked body was lying in a reservoir; a young woman with bruises that pointed to a painful end. Her dark hair hid her face, but I knew her name was Amy. Louise was asking me to tell her anything; anything at all would do.

"Louise, if I can be of any help, the best thing you can do is pray for the family. You can call the police in your town and tell them I will be more than willing to work with them directly. I will give you the name of the detective I work with. Or give my name to Amy's parents and ask them to call me directly, either way."

Louise wasn't that easy to put off. She stayed on the phone, demanding to know why I wouldn't talk to her about what I thought.

I continued, "There is no point in me discussing any of this with you. What is there to be gained by my surmising with you? You can't do anything with it, can you? Please just do what I said, and I will help all I can."

The next day I went out to my driveway to pick up my newspaper. I rarely looked at one; this was more in support of the town's paper. The headline read "Body of Amy Hoffman Found in a Reservoir in a Wooded Area of Randolph." As I read the account, it went on to say the body was fully clothed, and there was no indication of rape or any marks on the body. Why are they lying? How strange, what's the point? I knew she was already dead; what would be the reason they were publishing lies?

That afternoon, Detective Bill Hughes from the Mount Olive precinct knocked on my door. He was a huge man, about 6'5" tall and good-looking, with a wife who was blond, short, and very pretty. They had become my friends.

"Bill, why are they lying about Amy Hoffman in the newspaper? I know she was naked, tortured, and raped."

He simply shrugged, "I have no idea. She was found in another town."

Days later, I called Bill. "He's coming out again to kill. I can't stand this." Each day I became more and more anxious. My dreams were filled with snakes and knives.

One evening a few days later, Bill called, "A woman just died. She was thrown out of a car on Route 80, heading west at a rest area."

Now a task force was formed with multiple towns involved. They had their first meeting. And when it broke up, they would then work in pairs. Bill picked a partner, Captain of Homicide in Parsippany, Jimmy Moore. They drove straight to my home. I opened the door, and Bill greeted me with, "Nancy, this is Jimmy; he's my partner for the new task force, captain of homicide in Parsippany.

Would you repeat to him what you told me about the Hoffman girl?"

I repeated everything I had told Bill earlier. He asked me if I knew anything else. I saw Jimmy turn to Bill. He was unreadable. A good homicide investigator usually is. Jimmy's comments were, "she's good." They asked if I would drive around with them. I collected my bag, made sure the kids were taken care of, and left. As we drove, I continued to receive more information, "He was in Florida in jail for murder, then he murdered someone while in jail. Wow, he is crazy. And so is the parole board who let him out. I bet New Jersey will be suing the Florida parole board. That is horrible. They are dead because thoughtless people on a board freed him. How could they?"Driving through a residential section in Randolph, we passed acres of woods. The color of autumn was still lingering on some trees. Suddenly I felt ice cold and said, "It's down that road."

They turned where I pointed, both of them dead quiet. A hush came over us as we entered a wooded area that opened up into an odd space. In the center of it was a water reservoir. In a trance, I walked near it and went down on my knees, pleading and crying for my life. The knife I saw in a hand was used to taunt and to kill. Looking at the killer's face, I drew his image in my mind. A flood of thoughts poured through as Amy flew into the light, and I took back my body.

Back in the car, images continued to flip into view and there was no escape. A foggy evening, dusky images of a slim, dark-haired man who grabbed Amy at knife point as she sat, getting into her car. His blue car was right next to hers. It had odd taillights. Not knowing why, but trusting my intuition, I turned to Bill and stated, "Drive to the next town."

We were in Chester now driving towards Mendham. Pointing to the police station, I asked to go in. I still didn't consciously have a clue as to what I was doing. Bill and Jimmy introduced me to the captain. Bill told the captain, "Listen to her; she is psychic; we vouch for her." I began, "You have an officer whose last name begins with C."

"I've got two," the captain responded.

"Not the soft C, the hard C."

"Oh, you mean Costanza?"

"Yes. He gave three motor vehicle tickets this summer to a man who came up from Florida. He used to live in Hackettstown. Now he lives in The Hollow in Morristown. He murdered at least two people in Florida and was wrongly released from jail. His first name is James; his last name is K.... itch, something long and Polish sounding. I cannot pronounce it. He's moderately tall, about 5'10", he's slim, he has dark hair, he's well known to your officer. He or his brother worked or works at a gas station. He's got blood stains and hair in his car, and he has not cleaned it."

The captain asked, "Are you serious?"

"Absolutely. You will have positive proof that he killed Amy Hoffman. He's got family up here, and he is well known as a very dangerous person. He's committed multiple murders. This is a serial killer. He will kill again unless you stop him now."

The captain thanked me for my information, and Jimmy and Bill left with me. We went back toward my house, talking and very excited that we had something to go on. All the while, I kept seeing James. I could see his face; I could see his eyes; I could describe his house. Not knowing what else to do, we decided to go to The Hollow. The Hollow is a gully between two hills in Morristown, where I believed James lived. When we arrived at The Hollow, we started driving around.

"It's a white narrow house next to a yellow one," saying out loud what the movie in my head was showing. I didn't know what street it was on, so we kept driving around, just looking. It came to me again that either James or his brother worked at a gas station, and he had access to several different cars. They asked which car was used in the murder. I could not name the model but was able to describe the car. I proceeded to describe a blue/green car with special taillights.

Days went by and Jimmy, Bill, and I were in contact by phone daily. Jimmy was in charge of homicide, and we were all wondering why we hadn't heard anything yet. Meanwhile, the prosecutor's office had a man in charge who was the prime investigator for this case. I had a strong feeling that there were hidden agendas with this investigator. Why didn't we hear anything? Then I felt the murderer, James K_____, was doing it again. I could feel it building. He was going to kill again if he was not stopped. I believed he had attempted to stop several more women and did not succeed. I endured sleepless nights, praying no more women were going to be his victims.

Bill and Jimmy asked me to go with them to where the second victim died. We drove to Route 80's rest stop, where Dierdre O'Brien had been thrown out of a car. When I arrived, they asked me what I saw. I showed them where a trucker was parked. I pointed to the entrance area. "It's him again; I see the same car. He threw her out of the car, and a trucker picked her up. I see her bleeding body as she kept banging on the door of the truck to get the truckers' attention. She died in the trucker's arms." As I spoke, I was moving to where I believed the truck was parked that night and re-enacting what happened. I could feel her hand banging on the door. Most of all, I felt her remarkable, incredible spirit that cared to save others from this same fate. I was moved by her light, her amazing spirit of concern for others while she was in agony and dying from knife wounds.

"Yes," they said in unison.

"She was driving on Washington Valley Road outside of Morristown, and she was run off the road by James' car," was the next vision. I went on to describe how she thanked the trucker with her dying breath.

"We are not on the case anymore. All information is to be turned over to the prosecutor's office for investigation." That was Jimmy sounding upset. Jimmy's statement left us in limbo. He would not say why, nor would Bill. It confirmed that something was very odd with the investigating prosecutor since the case was not over. I knew the chief prosecutor didn't like publicity referring to a psychic, yet he wasn't above asking the sheriff, "Could you ask that psychic about ____ case." I imagined it was either him or the investigator. I couldn't leave it alone. Finally, one night I called Dr. George Williams, Louise's husband. "You are a hypnotherapist, aren't you?"

"Yes. I have a conflict. I'm the hypnotist for the witnesses who saw the car the perpetrator was in at the abduction of Amy Hoffman. They attempted to describe the car."

"I need to undergo hypnosis and see if I can retrieve more information or find out if I'm mistaken. Bill Hughes is a detective on the task force; he will be with me, and we will record the session."

He then agreed. George, Bill, and I went into his living room to begin the hypnotherapy. I began to listen to George's soothing voice as he started to hypnotize me. He instructed me to go back to the person who was committing all these murders. The next thing I knew, I was watching a scene. I started to describe it to George and Bill.

"I see a small brown car with a hatchback. In the car, I see a man who is extremely wild-looking, frightening. It's not James. It's a big man with lots of hair. James did not have lots of hair, and this man was very broad, unlike James. I see a woman with pigtails sitting there, terrified. The next thing I see is the car pulling up to an intersection. The woman is running out of the car and losing a shoe. She runs to the car behind them, and the driver of that car gets out to help her. Then the man from the brown hatchback gets out with a knife and goes towards the other man and says, 'Get out of here!'" I continued with, "The man from the second car jumped back into his car and pulled away as fast as he could. Now the only thing I see is an American flag on the corner."

I pulled myself out of the hypnotic state at this point because I couldn't stand it anymore. It was horrible. I did not understand what I was seeing. This man may have been James, but he seemed much larger and just as terrifying. I did not understand what was going on. I got home at about 8:15 PM, exhausted and anxious to lie in bed and read. I got into a set of oversized, floppy pajamas, and climbed into bed. As I was getting in, the phone rang. It was Bill. "I'm picking you up."

"Why?"

"Abduction on American Road in Morris Plain."

I realized what the American flag in my vision meant. "I'll be ready." I was dressed in a minute and walking out the door as Bill pulled up. I got in the car, and we picked up Jimmy. We went into the Morris Plain precinct and Bill told the prosecutor, "I have Nancy

Fuchs (now Weber) with me."

Investigator Russ Vanderbush: "Get her out of here. I don't believe in her!"

Jimmy: "If you don't listen to her, I'm leaving."

While we drove around, Bill mused, "There are probably a lot of people, not just officers, who have the ability but don't realize it. They may visualize something happening, but when it happens, they just shrug it off as a coincidence. Officers could probably be trained. Law enforcement ought to utilize this. There are so many cases that run into dead ends, but they are not dead cases. As I see it for myself, I wouldn't use it on a real strong case. Something that was cut and dried. If I had a case with no leads or with too many leads and I had to weed them out, it comes in handy. You don't want to be spending weeks chasing useless leads when your good leads are going cold on you. The longer it takes to solve a case, the harder it is." I couldn't agree more.

We spent until about 5:00 or 6:00 AM driving all over, searching for these people. Exactly what I had seen in my vision was reported to the police by the man who tried to help the abducted woman who attempted to flee from the brown hatchback. He had come running into the Morris Plains Police Department yelling about the man with the knife and the brown hatchback. They went to American Road, where they found a woman's shoe. They never found her; they never found him. There was no report of a missing woman. The three of us believed it was probably an unreported domestic violence incident. We searched all night, and I ended up with a 105-degree fever. I had never seen so many police helicopters in the air or police cars on the road as I had on that night. They came from every surrounding county, and some were even from Pennsylvania. They sealed off every road in the area, but he was gone. He was probably parked right under their noses somewhere and was most likely at home with her, killing her. After that, I thought, *I don't know what's going on.*

Since 1975, I have held a Thursday evening class in my home, where we meditated, studied a spiritual issue, and did metaphysical exercises. I had a group of people I knew very well coming to class that night. I told them about what had been going on and that it was totally confidential, not to be discussed outside of the room. I told them I was very confused about what was going on.

We all joined hands, and I spoke out loud to God that, "If it does not interfere in any sense, and if it is within the spiritual path of all, including the murderer's spiritual path, have him feel the pain that he has given to others, particularly the pain he keeps giving to women. Bring back to him, God, the mirror of his own feelings, and have him feel it all himself, and make him come forward."

The next morning, Jimmy called me and asked, "What did you do, Nancy?" I told him what I had done in class, calling on God to make this murderer feel his own feelings, and maybe turn himself in. He told me that a man had called for an ambulance and claimed he had been stabbed by a dark-haired woman who ran him off the road. The ambulance was sent, and the police were called in. They proceeded to come to his car where he waited, and found he had knife wounds in his back, which they later realized were self-inflicted. When the police looked over the car, they also realized it was a very similar car to the one I had described. He was taken in for questioning and put into custody. They obtained a warrant to search the car, and sure enough, they found Amy Hoffman's hair and blood inside. He was convicted of murders. His name is James Koedatich, and he is of Polish descent. The one thing that I saw throughout the whole thing, which was very peculiar, was that James always had a long mop of hair in my visions; except, every time I would work with my vision for a few minutes, he would lift it to reveal very short hair with a high widow's peak. It turned out that when he was brought to jail, he shaved off all his hair but left a high widow's peak. Yes, he did murder in Florida and went to prison, where he murdered his cellmate. The parole board let him out, and he came up to his hometown, Morristown, NJ, where he used cars from his brother's gas station. For me, this crazily sad event didn't end there.

Many years later, I hired a bookkeeper, Monica. One day she walked in with a box. Monica: "I saw a TV show last night with you helping on the Koedatich case. I had no idea you were involved. I worked for Joe O'Brien, who was Dierdre's father. He was best friends with Trumbell, the chief prosecutor who said that he should never have rotated Russ Vanderbush as the next up for a homicide case. He had never handled a homicide before. During that time, Trumbell felt so bad that he gave Joe all the inside information on the case. I was the transcriber since Joe wanted to write a book on what happened. Then Joe decided he would rather create a center in Morristown. That's the Dierdre O'Brien Center. He told me to do whatever I wanted with all the material. Here, Nancy, it's yours." She handed me the box with all the proof of everything I had reported.

Officer Costanza had called in the ticket to the investigating prosecutor in charge who "blew it off," saying he had already looked at him and now Captain Costanza continued with, "I kept that ticket in my desk drawer for years. I was so upset." Several women had narrow escapes with the killer chasing their cars after both Amy's and Dierdre's murders. While filming the first episode for Court TV's *Psychic Detective* series, retired Captain Jimmy Moore and Lieutenant 1st Class William Hughes and I took a lunch break together. Jimmy had retired and was free to talk. He finally told me how odd it had been. In all his years of work, when a task force is created, they all meet and share. This was the only time that did not happen. The investigator and one captain went behind closed doors to talk, while all the other partnering officers who gathered were not permitted to discuss with the investigator nor be told what was being reported to the office. I always thought the title for a movie on this case should be "Ego Kills." Over five towns called in to the office; they suspected James Koedatich. He blew them all off.

Exercise: Reaching into the Flames

If after reading "Serial Killer" you are moved to help, forge ahead with me. When you know a dangerous or scary situation has caught your attention, either indirectly or directly, use a vision of a GOLDEN HALO above your head. Now. Imagine the halo showering golden light down, eventually covering you in a cocoon of gold. This is a psychic shield as depicted in many master's paintings of Jesus, Moses, the Disciples, Mother Mary, and other sainted figures. The Hebrew word for horns is the same as for rays of light, so some painted Moses with horns and some with a halo; I like the halo!

Think of colors as varying wavelengths of light. Gold acts as a shield against lower vibrations of light. It produces a boomerang effect. Negative thoughts and ideas sent to the spiritually focused, shielded person boomerang back on the sender. This is the power of the universe, bringing you into its loving fold, reminding you of the Oneness.

Keeping ourselves in a most positive state, with spiritually oriented thoughts and feelings, not only protects us from some of the outside destructive forces. It also serves to boost our immune system and guides our intuitive decisions to be useful in the moment.

Play with this idea until it is easy and natural. Now, use it when you know you are going to be with someone who is usually draining. If you are around them for more than four hours, repeat the exercise. It only takes a minute, and no one needs to know. Notice afterward how your energy feels. Are you less emotionally spent? Take note of what you notice, reinforcing healthy change.

Go at your own pace. No one can judge it for you. A situation you know of that brings you to fear or tears requires reaching into your intuitive heart. Let the spark become a powerful flame of belief and caring. Bring the halo around you and then around all others, even those you fear. Miracles are what we are aiming for, so don't hold back; give it all you've got and watch the changes within you and, perhaps, the coincidental changes in the situations.

"Those doing soul work, who want the searing truth more than solace or applause know each other right away." – Rumi.

Chapter 10

UNSOLVED MURDER

"Mom, it's Ross English," Rebecca called out from the kitchen.

Walking into my bedroom, I wondered what was going on in town that he would be calling about. I didn't feel anything significant locally. She hung up as Ross began telling me,

"I just got a call from Warren County's Detective Bureau. Lt. Joseph (not his real name) is a friend; we go way back. He's heard we've worked together on a few things and knew I could reach out to you. Remember reading about a girl's body found in Washington Township a few months ago?"

"No, you know I don't read newspapers, I don't watch TV, and I absolutely avoid conversations about that stuff. If I'm going to work on something, I'd rather go in cold."

"I told Joseph that. He's hoping you will help him on that case. They have reached a dead end. You interested?"

"Sure, tell him I'll do whatever I can."

Lt. Joseph called a few hours later. Pleasant sounding man, not tough at all. Warm and friendly. Yet, I could feel a determination and dedication coming through, far greater than exhibited by many I had met. He gave me directions, and I gulped; an hour each way. No pay was offered, and I would be paying for my own transportation. The need to serve outweighed the "how will I put food on the table for my kids." I sent a plea to the Creator to support my children's welfare and got in my car. Although their police station was in a rural area, it had all the finesse that ours didn't. It was a large stone building in the center of town. The town had only a four-block radius, so it was easy to find. The lawn around the station was immaculate. Everything appeared clean, neat, and orderly–until I got to the detective bureau. I don't know what it is with them; the intensity of the job, the high from the donuts and coffee, the subconscious desire to bury the burden. Whatever it is, I've never seen an orderly office.

"You must be Nancy. Hello, I'm Lt. Joseph." His warm handshake matched his voice.

"I don't know how you work," he said. "I've never done this before. Can I get you something to drink?"

"Coffee, please." Why not join them on their speed trip?

"How do you take it?"

"Light, no sugar, thanks."

Lt. Joseph motioned me to a wooden seat by his desk, where I waited for his return. Chaos on his desk too; just like mine. I always thought I could find any paper I needed and was proud of that ability. I wondered if he was delusional like that.

"Here's your coffee. I'd like you to meet two other detectives we will be working with. They'll be back in a few minutes. One's at the lab and the others in court."

"No hurry, I can start on my own if that's all right with you. All I want to start with is for you to confirm that this is a murder of a female. Yes?"

"Yes. I have an object that belonged to her. Would you like to see it?"

Lt. Joseph was seated at his desk. He opened a drawer and pulled out a small plastic Ziplock, like the ones jewelers use. In it was a piece of jewelry. He handed the bag to me.

"May I take it out of the bag? "

"Of course."

Opening the bag and turning it upside down into my left palm, a thin gold-colored chain with a small cross lay in my hand. A dead girl's necklace. Getting my mind to stop thinking, I asked, "Is there somewhere I can go to sit alone quietly?"

"Right this way."

Following Joseph, I kept my eyes focused on the hall and building, not letting my mind get scared of the feelings and visions starting to surface.

"Here we are," Lt. Joseph said as he opened the door to a small chapel. Perfect.

"Thank you; I can find my way back to you when I'm done. I won't be long." Closing the door quietly, he left me to myself. Now I can let go and work. Praying for guidance, I held the necklace, still in my left hand. Slowing down my breathing and concentrating on the sound of my breath, I forgot where I was or what I was doing there. Good. This was a perfect place in which to work.

"Tell me about this girl," I directed my subconscious. "Tell me about this girl," I repeated those words several times and then stayed still, watching the dark screen that covers my mind. An image started emerging within seconds. A slightly built, long-haired girl was being chased in a cemetery by a very large red-haired man whom I knew was named John. As she fell, he picked up a stone and bent over. He proceeded to forcibly beat her head until there was very little left of it. I kept watching, looking for more clues as to who they were and anything about him I could see. His beard was darker than his hair. Pennsylvania, he lives there. She's a runaway.

Her thoughts started penetrating my mind. "Don't want my family to know what happened to me. I'm so ashamed of what I did when I ran away. Don't tell them."

"Who are they?" I whispered to the girl.

"Don't tell them. I picked him up. I needed the money. I didn't know he was so bad. He's crazy. I'm terrified."

"Do you know what he did to you?"

"Yes, he raped me."

"More than that. Do you know where you are now?"

"I'm here."

"Hi, I'm back." Lt. Joseph was talking with two other men seated by his desk.

"This is Nancy," Joseph said as he turned to me, "David and Robert are the other guys on the case."

"Want me to freshen your coffee?" Robert asked.

"No thanks, I usually sip from the same cup all day long. Don't want too much caffeine in me. Want to hear what I saw?"

"All ears." That was David.

All three of them looked interested. I would, too, if I had a case like that and absolutely no evidence and no leads. Taking a deep breath and wondering what I would say, I started, "She died last year. Her remains are not enough for absolute identification. She was about 15 at the time of death, about 5"1", slight build with long dark hair. Her killer has killed several times. His first name is John, short last name, one syllable beginning with an R. I hate to think it, but he may continue his rampage for quite a while. She picked him up. Because of this, there is difficulty in finishing this case. She feels ashamed of her lifestyle and stuck in her shame. Even though her body is dead, her mind is continuing, and she does not want anyone she once knew to know what happened to her. Her killer weighs over 220 lbs., is in his mid-30s, he wears a western belt buckle, has a scar on his cheek, and killed her with a stone or something like that, repeatedly hitting her head. I saw them running in a cemetery."

I continued to relate everything I saw. I left out the part where she and I made contact. I didn't want to lose my credibility over something I may believe can exist, but they may have a hard time understanding. This wasn't the place to argue philosophy or physics.

"I don't know how you could possibly know what we know, but you do. All true, except, of course, the description of the killer. It may be true, but we don't know." Lt. Joseph turned to the others and waited for their response.

"What do we do next? Do you think driving around the area might help?" David offered.

"Where's here?"

"Here, with you." Trying to be gentle, I went on. "Are you sitting down next to me?"

Her voice changed, "I don't know."

"How old are you?"

"Fifteen, I ran away at 13."

"So many years on your own. That's sad. Do you remember John chasing you in the cemetery?" Suddenly, pain erupted all through me, and I knew she had made the connection.

"He killed me. Oh my God, I'm dead. How can I be? I don't get it."

"We are talking through our souls. I'm sorry, I don't know how else to help you see. I can help you adjust if you like."

"Oh God, please do something! This is horrible; all I see is that stone." I could feel her terror as she sent her message to my soul.

"I know, you are so traumatized that you've become stuck. I'll do what I can. What name do I call you?"

"No, no name, my parents are not going to find out. No name, please do something. How can I go on?"

My eyes still closed, I called on the universe to bring a loving guide to take her across to the light. In my mind, I saw a woman I had seen before. She was carrying a bouquet of flowers, and she offered them to No Name. No Name took them and started to cry. The woman put her arm around No Name and led her away, down a path to a very bright light. The image stopped, and I became acutely aware. Aware of the wood pew I was sitting on, the sounds in the corridor, and the sickening feeling of having just experienced a murder. I opened my eyes, put the necklace back in the bag and left the chapel. Walking down the corridor, I came to the same office I had entered a half-hour before. So much had changed, though. No longer a stranger, I was part of the team. I felt a part of everything there, and now, probably as frustrated and upset as any of the other folks on this poor girl's case.

"Couldn't hurt," was all I could say. Driving out of town, I sat in the front seat with David while Robert and Lt. Joseph sat in the back.

Lt. Joseph said, "We named her Princess Doe. Don't know why but Jane Doe doesn't seem enough. We're hoping that with enough press attention, some more information might come up,"

We were passing a shopping center and I asked if we could pull in.

"I want to go into the pizza place."

"Sure, we could all use a drink. You hungry?" Robert asked.

"No, I think they were in here. Have you checked it out?"

"No," was Lt. Joseph's reply. Walking in, I slowed my pace down so I could feel the imprint of past energy lingering in the place. I stared in the air. Slowly, a haze appeared, and then I saw them, briefly, less than a second, then it was gone. They had been here the day of the murder.

"Done. Got what I need," I said as I started walking out. They were ordering drinks when I spoke. I walked outside; I needed different air. They followed me.

"Come up with anything?" Robert asked as he walked me to the front door of the car.

"Not much, just that they were in there that day."

"We can question the owner and workers later," David said as he took his notebook out and wrote in it. We drove out of the parking lot of the shopping mall, made a left to head further west, and I turned my head to the right. A group of stones caught my eye, all in a row... a cemetery.

    The pizza parlor was less than a block from the cemetery. They surely were there. How horrible. One minute pizza, next, terror and death. What a sick world. Sure enough, David pulled up by the cemetery. It was definitely the one I had seen in my vision.

"Just let me walk around by myself," I said as I moved out of the car.

I didn't want any interfering thoughts, and I hate preconceived notions of what happened; they're usually wrong. If I'm going to find out anything, I have to keep an empty mind and let the truth pour through. As I walked around the cemetery, I suddenly felt frightened of a clump of trees in a far corner, away from the road. Walking over to it, I felt like running far away, but instead, I got firmer and more determined with each step. I can't believe how frightening left-over energy can be. It was right by a ravine. The energy of the event was still around. I felt him throw her down into the ravine at the far end of the cemetery.

There it is, the same image, only this time, I'm looking up at a face. His scar on his right cheek; it's staring at me/her, this thing that is taking pleasure in my/her pain. My head…couldn't take the pain. I hurriedly walked over to the three guys. They felt like home—safe, secure. When detectives, who reek of the negativity and pain they are constantly exposed to, feel comfortable to hang out with, I'm in trouble. Most detectives start turning cold early or create a distance from the situation, which is what I needed. These three were comfortable with their own choices in life and were kind, thoughtful, and dedicated. A very wonderful mix to be with at that moment. As I noticed that, I remembered that each of the law enforcement officers I had come to know well were of the same mind. Thoughtful, courteous, respectful, and kind.

"Not getting much. He chased her back to those trees. The only other thing I can make out is a scar on his cheek, his beard, and a western belt buckle. The scar is deep; you can't miss it." I was speaking and walking back to the car, moving quickly to leave Princess Doe's death scene.

The rest of our conversation was a repeat of earlier ones, going over and over every detail in case we missed something. Heading back, I realized I still had another hour's drive ahead of me. My whole body joined my mind in exhaustion. I hardly spoke to them, and they seemed lost in their own troubled thoughts. Saying goodbye at their parking lot, I was grateful to slide into my wagon and be alone.

All the way home, I kept seeing his face, his eyes filled with a strange longing. The closest translation of that longing I could come up with was a longing to never be forgotten, to own another soul, to ensure the memory of their own existence at any cost, and above that, a pleasure in delivering pain as if that brought him power. With every blow, he felt more and more alive.

Shaking my head to move my thoughts, I put my radio on to a lively rock station. Fortunately, it was a song I knew. Joining my voice to the song, I started a new rhythm in my mind, letting the past recede as I grabbed hold of a different feeling through the lyrics. By the time I reached home, the visions were vague enough that they were no longer interfering with my ability to function.

Absolutely nothing came of that day's information. Lt. Joseph kept in touch, hoping I'd deliver some more precise clues, but I didn't. The case remained unsolved and open until July of 2022 when the victim was identified as Dawn Olanick, a then 17 year old runaway. Her killer, already in prison for murder, confessed. John Reese, who died in prison October 2021 was never questioned.

Exercise: Inner Detective Gets to Work

Create a program with your Inner Detective, where you ask yourself a lot of questions. As in taking a test, if you get a quick thought that seems to answer the question, grab it. If nothing comes or a jumble, let it go for now. Let's say you want to be able to be useful, but you don't know how.

For the Princess Doe case, here are some of the questions I asked my Inner Detective:

1. How old is she, child, teenager? The thought was yes to teen. How old? Numbers jumped around, 13, 15, maybe 16. Consciously I figured 15 was the average of what I was feeling.

2. When in the car, I pretended I had a simple map in my head that pointed left, right, up, and down. Sometimes I don't see a map; I feel drawn towards the right, straight ahead, left, or back. Think of us as electromagnetic (we are). A very subtle magnetic pull can happen when we focus on "where was/is the…?" If we are emotional when doing this, we stop being able to feel the pull or see the map.

I felt a pull "To the right" on this case. That took us to the far end of the cemetery. "Down"— that was the ravine.

3. When the important things occur like "Where did Kathy lose her engagement ring?" I felt my map pointing north in a home. That meant upstairs. Sometimes, I see in my mind; sometimes, it is simply a feeling that I accept. I accept it to build up the trust, even if it isn't correct. That one took a year before there was an answer. Patience and letting go of needing to know the outcome helps us live with the work.

Keep the ideas flowing; build a trust that you and everyone around can develop the ability to reach into that wondrous infinite flow of wisdom and information as long as we back it with love and respect. Respect for both ourselves and others can allow us to find peace, even when the outer world seems to struggle with that notion.

"If the doors of perception were cleansed, everything would appear to man as it is, infinite." —William Blake.

Chapter 11

IS HE A SERIAL KILLER?

Opening the door, I greeted Marge, my next client. She seemed inordinately sad; a great deal of grief was covering her. Her eyes told me she could not live well with a past deed and was here to change it. I brought her some water, and we went into my office. I like to kick my shoes off when I work; it's like rolling up my sleeves to get ready for hard work. Shoes at the side of my chair, I was braced for the worst. Here sat a sweet-looking woman, who by the condition of her hands and general appearance, seemed to work hard for a living. Her hair, slightly unkempt; she wore it in two braids. Her general look was that of being exhausted by life. I took a deep breath and plunged right in.

"You had a tragedy in the family. Your sister died recently?" I asked. Tears and a nod said enough.

"She was murdered?" Another nod.

As I spoke, a sequence of images came to me, too brutal to share. I saw a man beating a woman tied to a bed. There were details to the image that were so difficult to keep because it was all I could do to not let Marge see my reaction. She didn't need any more distress.

"Your sister worked in a hospital, hard worker, and in general, was kind and loving. She had a boyfriend who really cared. He is a sweet man and is devastated. He is a suspect, but Marge, he's not involved at all. The cops on the case are looking at the men in her life, and it isn't them. It's not a crime of passion or anything of that sort at all. This is a serial killer." I had said all I wanted her to know.

"Would you be willing to talk to the detectives who are working on the case?" Her voice was slightly hoarse. Cigarettes and recent crying had done that.

"Just give them the information and tell them to call Detective Lt. English for verification of who I am. You shouldn't have any problem. I think we'll get him. It feels like he is ready to stop and be caught."

She didn't ask what I meant, and I didn't explain. I was surprised at my own words. I'm not prone to giving predictions, especially on the outcome of something so serious. We chatted about the changes it brought to her family. Her shoulders seemed a bit straighter and stronger when she left, her eyes filled with less horror, more hope.

The next day a detective named Dave called. "Remember me?" he asked. "How could I forget?"

David continued, "Beas' sister came here telling us she had talked to a psychic. This always scares me because we get all these supposed psychics calling us. She went on and on. I asked her where this psychic lived, and she told me she lived in Flanders. I asked if she was Nancy (Weber) and she said that was who it was.

"Okay, Now, I'll listen. I went through police academy training when I received my badge. It was so obvious that psychology was lacking in the training. It's scary. Sometimes a cop turns out to be a bad guy. Perhaps they should have been psychologically tested in the beginning.

"Training as a psychic, also, is not so far afield from the study of psychology. You can certainly show people ways to get into their own subconscious. Maybe someday you'll be able to teach us the how-to's—but for now, I'm asking, will you work with us?"

A few days later, I was walking into Beas' apartment with Robert and David. Her apartment was on the first floor with a staircase at the entrance leading to another apartment. I looked up the stairs and shivered. Something up there was definitely disturbing. I saw a form, translucent and vague, on the staircase. It was a young, very thin male, about 19 years of age. He was mentally blocking my vision of what was upstairs, as if he was hiding something or someone.

Entering Beas' apartment, it was eerie to see everything exactly as it was on her last day on earth. Walking around the living room, I was taken by the beautiful shades of blue she chose for her chairs and couch, dark-hued but bright and comfortable. She was neat, nothing out of place. Her kitchen was small. I kept walking around it, sensing another presence. Three steps, and I'd turn around, finding myself back at the entrance to the living room. Someone had been in the kitchen.

Whoever it was, she knew him. Not her type. She liked sweet men, giving and kind. She had a boyfriend who was more on the shy side, quiet and caring. No, this man felt nothing like her boyfriend. As I walked towards the bedroom where I knew she died; the vacuum was in the living room. "He used the cord of the vacuum to tie her up," I muttered.

Time to go in. Robert and David were quietly walking behind me, staying out of the way, giving me plenty of space to do whatever I do.

Walking into the bedroom, there was no escaping the sight that waited. I walked to the left side and stared at the blood all over the wall by the head of the bed. Her blood only, none of it his.

He left her none. The sheets were covered with blood, I kept staring, hoping to remove myself from the present horror and back into the real one where it came from. Then I saw it. She was tied to the bed, wrists tied behind her, mouth covered with tape. He had a hammer in his hand, and he repeatedly brought it down on her head. Enough, I couldn't look anymore. I walked around to the other side.

"I think I've seen enough. Let's go somewhere else. "

Now, we were in their office, and a guy named John, with a one syllable last name beginning with R, was busy occupying my vision. David responded with, "No, can't be, what about her boyfriend, Joe? We think he did it. He was supposed to come over that night at 8:00 PM and claims he was tired and didn't go there that night. 11:00 AM the next day he walked in and found her."

"He's not lying; he called her to tell her he was too tired to see her. There's probably a record of the call. He was tired; that's probably why the killer got in. She knew him, but he was not someone close to her. Are you sure there is no one with red hair?" I insisted.

"Well," David chimed in, "there's her upstairs neighbor, but he doesn't have a scar on his cheek, and he doesn't wear a western belt buckle. At least I've never seen it."

"I saw a red-haired, bearded guy, name's John, scar on cheek, overweight, bulky, large western belt buckle, always in dungarees. Go back and look. He's the one, and he does have a scar on his cheek. He killed her with a hammer. Repeated blows to the head. True?"

David looked at me with a strange question in his eyes. "Yes, it was a hammer. We can't find it. Do you remember giving the same description for the killer of Princess Doe five years ago?"

"I vaguely remember. The same one, same style of murder, both women's heads crushed. I always thought he was a serial killer. Please question her neighbor."

"We did," Dave continued. "He passed a polygraph."

"That's because he didn't lie. You mentioned to me she died around 11:00 PM, I don't believe that's true. She died hours later."

Dave persisted, "What about her ex.? He lives in Florida but is a strange guy with a record."

"Absolutely not, zero interest in her. Besides, he can prove where he was that night. I'm telling you, go look at her upstairs neighbor." The rest of our conversation was friendly chatter while I gathered myself again for the ride home. The call came from David two days later.

"I didn't remember the scar on the cheek, and your insistence made me curious. Scar on cheek, western belt buckle, it was all there. We had started looking into him right after the murder.

We brought him in for fingerprints. We had a fingerprint from her window. We had brought in a windowpane and compared them. We kept picking John Reese up to talk to him because the guy I was working with had a bad feeling about the story he was giving. It just rubbed him the wrong way for whatever reason. As we kept going over Reese's story with him, we found more and more inconsistencies. We found out many things were not true. We even polygraphed him. He passed, and we eliminated him as a suspect for a while. I still felt there was something wrong with this guy. Based on what you stirred in us, we brought him in and videotaped our conversation. He gave it up and fully confessed."

Many months later, David told me, "After all this was over and he was convicted, we realized he was only giving us the story until about 11:00 PM the night the homicide occurred. When we polygraphed him, we realized we didn't take him far enough into the early morning, and he wasn't lying about the events up until that time. If we had taken him beyond 2:30 AM, we would have gotten him right away. Your description and input led directly to our bringing him in."

Exercise: Be a Practical Psychic

This exercise is for anyone, from the beginner to the serious investigator. Begin by finding three items that were not originally yours, but are now in your possession. As you may have gathered, it can be anything, from a handmade item to a cherished piece of writing, an unopened envelope or a trinket. The more energy someone else has used to either create or hold onto the item, the easier it may be to feel the history that now lies in its energy field.

Once you have collected the items, take them to a quiet space. Keep a journal or have a recorder available. You don't need more than a few minutes. Holding one at a time in both your hands, close your eyes, and let yourself observe what your experience is. Each of us receives the universal flow differently. No two snowflakes are alike, and neither are we. Some of us find ourselves getting clear images while others feel and sense situations. It's also possible to feel something strongly with one item, get a flash of a picture with another, and hear a word or two with another. Here are some of the rules I've developed for myself. See if any of these suit you.

1. Always begin by forming some kind of internal statement that offers yourself over to the divine flow: A channel of healing, receiver and giver of the healing energies of the Goddess/God/Creator/ Universal Source of Life, etc.

2. Center by taking several deep, prolonged breaths.

3. Regardless of what we know about the item or its history or presume to know, we create a mental space where we hold no preconception about what we will find.

4. Keep the emotions aside for this brief time of work.

5. Record the findings, including the date, through writing preferably.

6. Record everything; the silly nonsensical meanderings, the body sensations, the mental chatter, visions, sounds, ideas, and any other observations of the experience during those few moments of centered, focused intention on an object, photo, or situation.

7. Remember, the harder we try, the more pressure we are applying. Pressure pushes away the subtle layers of information and energy. Think of them like soft clouds passing over the sun; wait, once they move, we can see!

8. Taking the work seriously does not mean forcing an answer; it does mean practice, practice, practice. Like dancing, singing, painting, playing, swimming, and getting into the "Zen head," the oneness with the process takes time and patience.

9. Finally, I find that a little knowledge of symbolism helps.

    What you "get" or see with the mind's eye may be "as is" — literal. It can be a pun, a symbolic idea. The sun setting can mean you go somewhere where you see a beautiful sunset or move to an area where that is a prominent view. Or it can be a symbol of an ending of a situation…or? Consider asking yourself, is this "as is," or is it symbolic? Write it all down.

    The wonderful thing about being wrong is that eventually, you get to know the difference between the literal and figurative information that comes through—if you write it down. Writing will give you a clear map to channeling universal knowledge. It's exciting to discover your own ability to learn directly from our Creator.

"The art of writing is the art of discovering what you believe."
—Gustave Flaubert.

Chapter 12

NO ANSWERS

It can take me years to feel free to author a nonfiction crime story. Either it hasn't been adjudicated, the police officer will be in trouble if their superior knows I've worked the case, unrevealed details may endanger someone, or I'm not told the outcome. Since I don't keep up with crime news and most people I work with believe I already know what's happened, I walk away from the work knowing I've done the best I can and leave it at that. When I work locally, it's a lot easier to find out what has happened. Even then, some of the salient facts known years before by others come up casually in a catch-up conversation as "Remember when we found the hammer you mentioned?"

"No, I didn't know you found it." That was my reply then, and for several other similar conversations. This story is purposefully disguised to protect the innocent, including me.

Three FBI agents were assigned to a double murder investigation. Because of their responses to me, I mentally nicknamed them Dreamer, Skeptical and Curious. I was asked to fly out of state where the double murder had been committed the previous year. The FBI had worked on the case and come up empty. The family called me in, and the FBI agreed to work with me for a day. They were all waiting when the taxi pulled up and dropped me off. The three FBI men were pleasant and fairly open. One emphatically told me he was skeptical, one that he dreamt of me the night before, and one was simply curious. For first timers with a psychic, I thought they were pretty easy to be around. The home they took me to was where a double murder occurred. It had an open space for a living room and kitchen with a long hall leading to other rooms. Once we were in the door, I needed to explain my approach.

"I know you haven't a clue how I do what I do or if I can. Here's what I need. I'll walk around and tell you things I feel, hear and see. You will please confirm or deny they mean anything to you. Okay?"

"Sure," said Curious. "Do you want to see photos of the scene?"

"Not now. Definitely not now. Please don't lead me in anyway; in fact, just take some seats and let me lead myself. Afterward, I'll certainly look at any material you want me to see."

Walking to the half wall that was the boundary between the kitchen and living room, I sat on the floor and stared at an image of a man in his mid-30s. He talked slow, not southern slow, slow as in difficulty putting words and sentences together. I felt a sweetness about him. I plunged ahead.

"I see a man lying against this wall. He died here. He was in his mid-30s, appears fairly tall and slow-minded, perhaps slight mental retardation. Very kind, very sweet. Mean anything?"

"Confirm," said the agent, who apparently, knew me in a dream. In my mind, I started thinking of him as Dreamer, rather than his name.

"Okay, he just told me a weird word I don't quite get, it sounds like a Swedish version of the word - jokes - like - yokes, that's it, yokes. What does that mean?"

Dreamer said, "It means nothing at all." They all concurred.

"Okay, let me go on then. We'll get back to that later. He is showing me he was shot in the back and fell. The gunman shot his father, who was down the hall trying to enter a room." "Confirm." They all agreed.

"The gunman took a satchel of money from the father's body. Oh, that's what the father was trying to hide. Then the gunman ran out to a black van that was waiting for him. That's all I'm getting here, other than the father died too."

"Confirm," said the group.

"I'm ready to follow the van unless you want me to look at anything else here."

"Could you look at the photos? Maybe something else will come to you." Curious handed me a stack of crime scene photos.

"Guys, why didn't you tell me that yokes were yolks—look, here are the two eggs he dropped when he died. He was telling me he dropped them. He felt bad about breaking them. Poor guy."

"What egg yolks?" They all came and peered over my shoulder. The photos were clear and sharp; so was the image of two egg yolks by the man's body. I understood from an earlier conversation that they were only on the case recently and had to pour through hundreds of papers. Impossible to remember it all.

I was the first to speak: "Can we go follow the black van I saw?"

We piled into the black sedan, me in the back with Dreamer, Skeptical and Curious in the front. Curious mentioned he had a transcript of the case if I wanted to see it. I was no longer considered an outsider, at least to two of them.

"Turn right at this corner, then just keep going straight for a while. I feel it will be a few miles of straight driving. Ah...he's not driving; he has a male friend driving, and they're talking. Bobby, that's the killer's name, and Ed is his buddy."

Skeptical was quick to point out: "No, that's not possible. We know of Bobby, and we questioned him. His alibi is shaky, but he was with a woman that day, not a man, and there is no one named Ed."

"His name is Ed. It's so clear. Bobby had a fight the day before with the older man he shot. Don't know why yet. Turn to the left here and then up by that crossroads, go right."

A few miles later, "Okay, turn right here, there...the trailers...he lives in that one."

As I pointed, they pulled in front of it. Now I was terrified we would be confronting a killer who would know who I was. I was so frightened I couldn't hear or see anything except my fear.

Dreamer spoke first, "You're right; you directed us straight to Bobby's trailer. We know him. We will question him in jail, that's where he is spending some time for a burglary. Hey, I'm ready to break for lunch; anyone else?"

Over lunch in a nearby diner, Curious handed me the transcript for review. I put it aside while we ate. Dreamer commented, "That was incredible; I never worked with a psychic before."

Skeptical responded, "I don't know. Look, Nancy, I don't mind working with you, but don't expect me to believe you know or do anything special."

My turn, "Fine with me. Bobby went into the man's retail store the day before he shot him and argued with him. Bobby is into black market stuff and wanted the guy to carry his products. The man refused. That's why he and his son are dead."

"Makes sense to me. We know they fought the day before. Customers saw Bobby talking with the old man in the back of the store, and they weren't being friendly." Dreamer was quick to concur.

We were back in the car, driving to the house again. "I'm going to read for a few minutes, see if anything strikes a chord." I started reviewing the transcripts. "Here's Ed! You guys... it's in the transcript!" I said as I handed them the page. "See? Bobby spoke of him the first time he was questioned. He simply lied and said Ed was with him the day before. How could he have been? Bobby was alone with the old man. He went alone. He changed the days around." Dead silence as they read.

Curious was first, "We're fairly new on the case. We read through, must have missed that. Now we have a strong lead and probably can break his lies. Thanks."

Dreamer handed me his card saying, "When you get back up north, call if you get anything else. I think we have enough to go on. Please don't talk to anyone else about this." That's the last I heard about the case. I have no idea whether they were able to convict.

Exercise: Everyone's a Channel

If you've done any of the exercises or have been doing things like this all along, you have learned that the power comes through us, not from us. Being able to control when we use this, what we use it for, when to keep quiet, and when to speak up. These are all part of the path and the mission. For anyone who is reading this and has no interest in pursuing this particular path, know that whatever you do in life needs the power to come through you.

Call it whatever you want. The blend of the divine powers, intelligence and intuition is a very heady mix. Like all gifts, it involves the same thing I mentioned throughout this book. The building of trust in your inner detective to receive direct knowledge from the Source of All.

So, what's the exercise? Trust yourself to be a channel. Call it whatever you want in whatever you do in life. A parent asking for inner guidance to help a child, a friend wanting to help a friend seek guidance for the highest good from the infinite source. Create a belief that entitles you to the same use of power that anyone can tap into.

Watch the magic!

"Following our inner guidance may feel risky and frightening at first, because we are no longer playing it safe, doing what we 'should' do, pleasing others, following rules, or deferring to outside authority."
—*Shakti Gawain.*

Chapter 13

BUNNY'S STOLEN!

The woman's voice was spilling frantically through the wire as she implored me to find her dog. Bunny was possibly stolen, and she was desperate.

"What is your name?"

"Sue, I'm from Ellicott City, Maryland. I'm sorry, but I'm absolutely desperate. Bunny means everything to me. I can't get around well. It's hard to go looking. I found your name in *Grit* magazine. You do find missing pets, don't you?"

"Sometimes, I'll do whatever I can to help."

My hand still held the telephone, and my feet still touched the floor, but something I call my being or essence was no longer in Budd Lake, New Jersey. I was traveling with the winds, faster than awareness. Seconds ago, Sue asked a question, and now, I'm staring out through the eyes of a beautiful, sweet German Shepherd. She reminds me of the first dog I had as an adult.

It was 1968. I was pregnant and married to a nightmare. We lived in Puerto Rico while my husband did research on brain functions. Two weeks after moving from the Bronx, Gil turned into a raging lunatic. He would slap or punch me, then, on bended knee, would cry and apologize. I learned that if I didn't accept his apology, another beating would follow. Being stranded on a beautiful island with no phone, no car, except when he relented to let me use it, and pregnant with complications was as close to hell as I ever want to get. Whatever mistakes and screw-ups I've made, that marriage and subsequent problems more than paid for any karma I'd accrued.

It was after one of his insane apologies that we went looking for a dog. When I walked into the breeder's home, a three-month-old puppy was brought out. Love at first sight is a habit with me, especially with animals. My "lamb" followed me everywhere; no training necessary. The minute Gil left to do research, my buddy jumped into the Gil-forbidden bed, put his head on a pillow, and cuddled with me. Mary and her little lamb never had it so good. We were inseparable from the first. Now, my buddy and Bunny were joined in my heart. Bunny seemed to have the same depth of devotion and sweetness. I ached for her. Suddenly aware of the voice on the other end. I answered, "The first thing I see is Bunny in Virginia. I see her being taken in a station wagon. There are two men in it. They feel like they just pulled a robbery. She is with a man with a shotgun. He is scuzzy looking. I see him on top of a hill."

"That's impossible. My car was stolen, but she's definitely not in Virginia. I live in Maryland, but I'm not near Virginia; that's quite a run. She can't be there. Please, I need your help. Can't you tell me anything else?"

"You had a station wagon?"

"Yes."

"Then I do see it. It's the first town over the border, going directly south of you. I can only tell you what I see. Bunny is a large German Shepherd, isn't she?"

"Yes, that's true. But I don't believe that someone would be able to drive my 13-year-old station wagon that far or that someone would travel that distance with such an old dog. Bunny is 12-years-old."

"That is what I'm seeing, I can't make up a new story because it doesn't make sense. I've learned to trust the images and impressions."

    The next day a breathless Sue began, "Bunny was seen in a station wagon heading south after a robbery with two men driving. The police think they were heading toward Virginia. How did you know? When will they find her? Is she okay?"

"Yes, Bunny is not hurt, but she'll be hungry and scared. I don't see the men harming her."

"How can you be sure?"

"I'm traveling there with my mind; that's how I can tell. No one is ever sure until we have proof.

Sue, I've been like this ever since I can remember. I'm so glad Bunny has you. You must love each other very much. Thanks for calling and keeping me informed. I'll be praying for her. Keep sending her loving thoughts. Keep your fears away from your thoughts of her. It's important. She's very telepathic and loving you; she is very sensitive to your thoughts."

"But how am I ever going to get her back? Where is she? She can't be in Virginia?"

"Why don't you send me a photo of her. In the meantime, until I get it, please work on letting some of the fear abate and remaining open to the possibilities I'm seeing. I could be wrong, I know, but I could also be right. Call me in a day or two."

The photos were on my desk two days later when her call came. "Hi Sue, okay, this time I see her by railroad tracks. Wait a minute, I think I feel a name coming...Harpers Ferry, West Virginia. Isn't that a movie or something?"

"Are you sure?"

"Yes, hold on, there are more images coming. I'm waiting for them to clear."

The images were barely there; like looking through a long tunnel to see a speck of something. Only you know the speck is the key to a mystery, and it's important to get a detailed shot and somehow enlarge it; translate into common sense and be right.

"There are mountains and water nearby. She's on a mountain, alone. She's waiting for you. You can find her. Sue, you are going to see a truck, wooden sides, color green, and there's a bandanna on the seat."

"Is that where Bunny is?"

"No, but it's a clue to tell you that you are on the right track. I think she is by the railroad tracks near the mountain. Poor girl, she misses you. You've been sending her a lot of good messages. I can feel her being comforted."

Sue called back with the good news. Bunny was in her arms again.

The visions were true. I turned to my buddy, now many years a spirit, "Thank you for keeping Bunny company, I love you. Just once more, I'd love to hug you. You kept me company in some of my darkest moments."

Exercise: Drench Yourself in Belief

Visions of success, along with the emotions that go along with the actual success, create a powerful magnet. It's taken me a long time to be confident, while knowing I may not be right. A funny and necessary recipe for handling some situations is to maintain this perspective. Whatever you are choosing to create for your path, consider these points while visualizing or doing a dream board or writing your affirmations and your goals.

Want to write a book, and you think, "that's ridiculous, I can't write?" I thought that years ago too. When I needed to say something, I wrote, disregarding grammar, and blasting through blocks. It was a hit and miss, mostly miss. Yet, because the visions I held were, I believe, important to share with others, I made sure I kept going with my vision work. I want you to promise yourself you will seek your own mission, your own passion for something you feel is worthwhile. Worthwhile can be cleaning houses for others who also have a mission that leaves them with few choices of free time, family, or cleaning. All productive work is worthy of being a mission. It is your energy exchanged with others for good reasons. I love the fact that there are great folks who collect our garbage. What would I do without them? Their mission frees my mission. Get it?

Write your goal, picture it vividly, get the emotions stirred in as if it's occurring now, believe it while you are working on it. Trust that your soul will guide you in the best direction for your spiritual fulfillment. Do this and perhaps someday, a call will come or an email asking for your help, and you will be ready to jump in, take the risk, call upon our Creator to guide you, and go for it!

If you want insight into how to communicate with our furry, feathered, finned, scaly, fine friends, read my book *All Nature Speaks, Conversations With Pets And Wildlife*, published in 2022, available at Amazon, with personalized signed copies available from *nancyorlenweber.com*

"Creativity is just connecting things. When you ask creative people how they did something, they feel a little guilty because they didn't really do it, they just saw something. It seemed obvious to them after a while. That's because they were able to connect experiences they've had and synthesize new things." —Steve Jobs.

Chapter 14

THOUGHTS ON

BEING A PSYCHIC DETECTIVE

Yes, Nancy Drew was one of my favorite characters to read about. So were Florence Nightingale and Clara Barton. Each one, excited by life, not only willing to help but compelled to help. The common thread was they couldn't stay away from helping; it was as important to them as breathing. Okay, Nancy Drew was made up, yet she still has influenced many of us.

I wouldn't be able to write this or be here if it wasn't for one of the hardest and strangest situations I've encountered. As a young nurse, I worked for my brother-in-law's uncle on Saturdays. He chose to work in a poor section of Brooklyn to give back to the neighborhood. He was generous, kind, compassionate, and willing to help me research, teach me how to take x-rays, and so much more. I knew if someone called who had no money and a sick child, I could tell them to come on in; it's free. One day his regular nurse called me at home.

"Nancy, my daughter is getting married, and I need the extra work to pay for it. Do you mind if I come in this Saturday instead of you?" "Of course not," was my quick response.

That fateful Saturday was the only time I did not work on a Saturday in a year. The call came that night from my brother-in-law. "Nancy, there has been a terrible tragedy. Two men came in to rob my uncle's place as they were closing up. One, shot and killed him, Dr. Milton Lopyan."

One man was easily found and sent away for life. The other was not caught. His assistant believed they did not shoot her because she was African American, and so were they. I'm not sure why she was saved; I only know she saved me from that horrible time. Perhaps there was a plan for me? Or I need to be forever, gratefully, making my life worthwhile for Milton and all the other victims who left this world before their time.

The greatest difficulty in this psychic detective work is obvious; you get to feel what the victim went through. The greatest gift is the possibility of helping to put closure on the situation for all involved and to prevent, if possible, future harm. Is it worth it? Of course. Does everyone who is psychic get a shot at working with law enforcement? Obviously not. And for obvious reasons, it isn't all about being psychic. It is also about being part of a team effort. Search your heart carefully. If a piece of the need to serve is about being known or proving yourself right or powerful, hopefully, you will work on that error of thought and belief before you work in crime. I believe that part of the role of the psychic in law enforcement is to open doors of understanding, not close them. Good, dedicated law officers are so committed to the calling that they work on their off time.

While psychics have been recommended as one of the tools for solving crimes, many officers are reluctant. Most don't know how to find "authentic" psychics. That's what they have told me, ones they can trust, not only to give them leads but, even more importantly, to not discuss open cases with people outside the investigation.

Several years ago, I was a part of a panel on the *Rickie Lake Show*. The panel was made up of people whose children were parentally abducted. The audience was also comprised of parents of abducted children. I was the resident psychic who had found missing children.

Somewhere in the midst of a man telling his story, I had a vision of his wife and his two-year-old son in Canada crossing into Michigan, going back and forth through the two countries. I kept quiet. When Rickie asked if I saw anything, I commented that some things are not appropriate for public shows. I then suggested that if everyone in the audience and at home watching would send their prayers for a safe return, more miracles would occur. We all make a difference.

During intermission, Rickie came over and said, "You saw something for that man, didn't you?"

Nodding in the affirmative, Rickie asked what it was.

"Rickie, I will be happy to tell him after the show and any investigator he works with. If too many people hear it, she may sense it and flee for good."

"Absolutely true. I promise not to tell anyone; can I listen?"

Trusting her, we agreed to talk later. I told the distraught man that in May (this was March), his ex-wife would be driving from Canada to Michigan with his son, and a customs agent would stop them. His son would be brought to him almost immediately, and she would be going to prison for several years. She had fled from their home when he discovered she was a prostitute who simply wanted to marry an American to continue her lifestyle in the US and earn more money.

In May, I received the wonderful news from the father. A blessed customs official at the Canadian/Michigan border didn't like her looks, pulled her over, and promptly discovered she was wanted. She received several years of prison time. The son was brought right back to his dad.

I didn't find them; I assisted in offering hope based on insight. Perhaps through the power of loving intention and vision, I added something to the prayers and beliefs that already existed, and that can only be of value.

I mentioned earlier my love for Florence Nightingale and Clara Barton. Being a medical intuitive all my life, I was shown the importance of synthesizing these gifts with my nursing career when a physician handed me a chart on a new patient. Without thinking, I said, "He doesn't have congestive heart failure, order an upper GI, he's got a very enlarged hiatal hernia."

"How do you know?" was the physician's reply.

"Because I see it, don't you?" I thought that's why everyone went into the study of healthcare. Aren't the problems in bold highlights in the energy? Fortunately, despite my being a brash 18-year-old fresh out of nursing school, he did it and thanked me when the results came back. That moment was the first time I can remember being happy about these abilities. That settled it. There was a purpose to this gift. I have followed my heart's calling to do no harm. It led to many new paths of study; homeopathy, herbs, nutrition, and for the last almost twenty years, essential oils. What we have been given to help ourselves fascinates me. I seek to support others in their need to support their lives, their mind/body, and most of all, to demonstrate gratitude for life by caring for all of life. While I still work on a few criminal cases, the parable that has guided me to focus now on educating others in both the metaphysical fields and the holistic lifestyle fields is this:

Two people are by the side of the river, pulling out drowning people. They never stop. It is a 24/7 task. One turns to the other and says, "We need to go to the head of the river and find out why they are falling in."

If your spirit is guiding you toward visions of painful occurrences, it is not to scare you or harm you. It is to let you know you have the power to help. Open your heart and your mind; let the Light that fills your life flow with purpose toward the visions you encounter. Be grateful for any help you give, through prayers, through actions, through thought. Be the Light.

May the blessings of the Great Spirit of Life be upon you,

now, and always.

May you find your calling each day of your life.

May your Spirit dream walk with power.

When powerful winds of hurt and pain are blown at you or in front of you, the spirit of your soul's connection to our Creator will keep you flying with love.

And may you and all your loved ones breathe deeply the vision of the

Light filled with love.

A big thank you for believing I have something of value to say to you.

I hope it has been of some help in your journey.

In the infinite light of love, Nancy

RESOURCES

My book "*All Nature Speaks, Conversations with Pets and Wildlife*" is available on various book sites (Amazon, etc.). Personalized signed copies are available at *nancyorlenweber.com*.

For information on classes, workshops, speaking engagements, and lectures by Nancy, please email nancy@nancyorlenweber.com.

My personal website is nancyorlenweber.com. There you will find:

One-to-one mentoring sessions for those looking to improve or tweak their gifts. Please look at the mentoring page on my website for further information.

On my blog menu read and play *A Gift of Music for Everyone* and *More Gifts of Music for Everyone*, music, and music overlaid with my voice guiding creative visualizations and meditation. (The original music of the "SuperLearning" form is used with permission from the authors of *SuperLearning*). It is free. Use it for relaxation and/or to increase focus.

At https://nancyorlenweber.com/essential-oils/ is information on some of the usages of essential oils. There you can see all the products. Why only the featured company? With 20 years of insight and oversight, I know they are the only ones I would ever use.

I use essential oils extensively as my daily go-to. If you have not used my preferred products and would like to experience their benefits, please email me for a complimentary private consultation. Email nancy@nancyorlenweber.com, Subject: Oils and Psychic Detective.

Intuition is assisted and enhanced with the use of quality essential oils and a healthy lifestyle. The essential oils, from soil, to seed, to opening the bottle, will harmonize with the frequency of your being. It was a choice for which that I am forever grateful. I thank the voice within that whispered, "Choose to be part of the Creator's creations."

For lay and professional healers, check out Lightwingcenter.org for classes, certifications, master instructor training, and more. If you are a lay healer and your state requires a "hands on" license to work, please read about our specific Holistic Practitioner Ordination. For nurses, we offer CE's and Certification for hands-on aromatherapy training.

Our holistic ministry's website is lightwingcenter.org

MORE RESOURCES

Judith A. Hancox, MSW, LCSW, BCETShttp://www.judithhancox.com/ offers helpful, trauma defusing suggestions, and grief therapy at www.shiome.com. Ms. Hancox does both in-person and phone consultations.

This OVC-funded database provides access to victims' rights, statutes, tribal laws, constitutional amendments, court rules, administrative code provisions, and case summaries of related court decisions. https://www.ovc.gov/rights/legislation.html

https://www.emdrhap.org/content/what-is-emdr/Trauma Recovery Therapy

https:// www.helpingparentsheal.org/

This is open to all who have lost a child. (Any age) Judith A. Hancox and I give talks for this organization along with many other mediums and therapists.

Comments? Email me at *nancy@nancyorlenweber.com* or go to my personal Facebook page, *Nancy Orlen Weber*.

If you are looking to connect for any work, please read nancyorlenweber.com as the first step.

If I don't respond to a request, please email me. I have someone else wade through Private Messages, Messenger, and whatever else may exist, so it is always best to also email.

Facebook   Psychic Detective Nancy Orlen Weber fan side

Instagram *@nancyweber372*

A BIG THANK YOU TO...

While I write alone, it has taken hours of my captive editor's time to help me gain more clarity and make my lunch, dinner, take me to the movies, dance with me, and so much more.

To my soul mate, Dick Weber, I love you forever and beyond.

Because one editor is not enough (grammar is my strong point not), Parker Novi, grandson extraordinaire, did a round of editing. I'm hoping he is my forever editor, which frees my husband to format, edit, come up with ideas, brainstorm, and in general, fill in the techie gaps that seem like a foreign language to me.

To Rebecca and Jesse, my daughter and son, who growing up were told, "I'm sorry I can't do what I promised, there's a missing child"... or other horrible things I couldn't tell them, you were my reason for caring about the entire world. My love for you spills over continuously to all else. I once mentioned to you, "If something happened and you were missing, I would want the world to turn around and help find you." You are amazing children whose compassion forgave me for breaking those promises and for staying as precious and loving as you are.

This books may point the reader toward a new beginning. If you are motivated by the stories and resolve to resonate with the positive outcomes that collective community generates, as exemplified in the Exercises in Nancy's books, you may want to add your power to the effort for good.

One way is to join Nancy in her online course

"Sacred Soul Powers",

where your Inner Detective can find effective voice to quell conflict *and* promote lasting peace.

Nancy Orlen Weber is well known Psychic Detective who enjoys extensive media exposure through many interviews and documentaries. She presents classes and workshops, and has done so for over 45 years, where she shares her techniques for developing spiritual outcomes.

Documentaries on Nancy's work with law enforcement demonstrate how her practical insights can be applied universally to all circumstances.

Nancy is a nurse, minister, author, wife, mother, grandmother medium, animal communicator and psychic.

Nancy's books *The Life* Of *A Psychic Detective* and her newest book, *All Nature Speaks* share her true stories and techniques to empower every ones' spiritual journey.

Developing Sacred Soul Powers

There is companion program aligned with Nancy's books and philosophy to amplify development of your Psychic Detective, built upon the foundation established in Nancy's books.

https://nancyorlenweber.com/contact-us/

Click on the drop down menu and choose

My Sacred Soul Powers

We Are All Seeds

This Blessed Planet,

a child no more nor less

created, with love and the greatest of prayers

This Earth longs for all to embrace the truth-

all are part of, and none stand alone

The rich, the poor, the in between,

The trees, waters, and all the kingdoms of life

Each is given the Seeds, each must care for the whole

Let us see all in the light.

Believe the Seeds are planted by listening to our Souls

Each Soul guided towards love

Keep steady in our hearts, keep love as the answer

Then we feel alive, as only love can do

The divine spark of life within all

The blossom is love, the nectar is peace,

and the fruit is fulfillment.

In the infinite light of love,

Nancy Orlen Weber

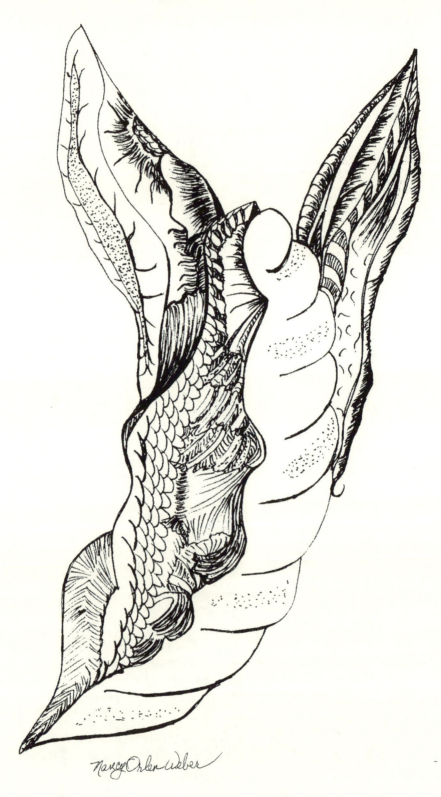

Made in United States
Orlando, FL
04 September 2023